Shame on You

Shame on You

How to Be a Woman in the Age of Mortification

Melissa Petro

G. P. Putnam's Sons
NEW YORK

PUTNAM
— EST. 1838 —

G. P. Putnam's Sons
Publishers Since 1838
An imprint of Penguin Random House LLC
penguinrandomhouse.com

Library of Congress Cataloging-in-Publication Data

Names: Petro, Melissa, author.
Title: Shame on you: how to be a woman in the
age of mortification / Melissa Petro.
Description: New York: G. P. Putnam's Sons, [2024] | Includes index.
Identifiers: LCCN 2023058460 (print) | LCCN 2023058461 (ebook) |
ISBN 9780593714997 (hardcover) | ISBN 9780593715000 (epub)
Subjects: LCSH: Shame. | Women—Conduct of life. | Women—Psychology.
Classification: LCC BF575.S45 P49 2024 (print) |
LCC BF575.S45 (ebook) | DDC 152.4—dc23/eng/20240520
LC record available at https://lccn.loc.gov/2023058460
LC ebook record available at https://lccn.loc.gov/2023058461

Printed in the United States of America
1st Printing

Book design by Silverglass Studio

Author's note: I have told my story truthfully to the best of my ability. Other people's stories were collected by email, over the phone, in person, and virtually for the express purpose of being included in this book. When requested, names and identifying details were changed. All stories were edited for length and, in some cases, clarity. I did my best to represent them accurately and offered each interviewee an opportunity to read their edited story prior to its publication. Additional research was conducted over the past twenty years, and I have done my best to ensure that each influence was recognized and properly credited.

For Molly

Contents

Shame
on You

Prologue

The National Arts Club buzzed with restless energy. Press milled about the members-only clubhouse, journalists draining bodega coffee from paper cups as February sunlight streamed through stained glass. I hovered alone in the shadows, clutching a printout of the speech Gloria Allred and I had worked on the night before.

All things considered, I looked good. The outfit, later described by the *New York Post* as a "virginal white mohair coat, navy-blue minidress, and brown sky-high platform do-me pumps," had come from the fast fashion outlet Zara. It probably cost two hundred dollars—significant to me, as I could barely pay for shampoo at the time, let alone new clothes.

Never mind what I could afford, it all felt essential, like armor. Standing at a podium that morning in the mansion-turned-clubhouse's former library, in front of an elaborate fireplace and surrounded by mahogany bookcases stuffed with leather-bound books, I was determined to not be what people thought of when they heard the word "prostitute." I wouldn't let them make me out as a victim, sitting on a bed with my face obscured, hands folded in my lap. Nor would I be the villain the media had spent the past six months painting me as.

People would see me, I hoped, for what I was: your average single white female, a thirty-year-old Midwesterner, one of countless transplants who'd moved to New York City for college and decided to stay. I was a writer and, until recently, had been a public-school teacher of art and creative writing at an elementary school in the South Bronx.

I was also a former sex worker. And to many in the New York press corps—and, it seemed, to my superiors in the New York Department of Education—my past as a dancer and escort and my current role as an educator were incompatible.

But was that the real issue here? Or was it maybe that I'd refused to stay silent about that past? Truth be told, I'd never been exactly secretive about it. It had never been an issue. I'd spoken freely about my prior sex work when I was in graduate school, among my friends, even to some of my teaching colleagues. But when I'd dared to get political and started raising my voice in a more public forum, the backlash had begun.

It started with an op-ed I'd published on the *Huffington Post* months before that criticized online classifieds Craigslist founder Craig Newmark's decision to cave to political pressure and remove the erotic services section of the website. I'd used my firsthand experience selling sex on the platform to support my argument that not all the women on Craigslist were underage or working for a pimp. And because I was also arguing that sex workers should be allowed a voice in the conversation about women's participation in the sex industry and be unashamed to speak for themselves, I'd signed my name to the piece.

That's when the frenzy began.

After the article ran, a reporter from the *New York Post* put two and two together, connecting my name to another essay I'd written months earlier in which I'd mentioned being a schoolteacher. The next morning I was front page news: BRONX TEACHER ADMITS: I'M AN EX-HOOKER.

The moment my employer got word of what was happening, I was banished from the classroom and hidden away in the infamous "rubber room"—a warehouse for teachers who were deemed too problematic to put in front of students but not able to be fired—while my case wound its way through the city bureaucracy.

All through that fall and winter, I fought hard to keep my job. But the fight was over. The press conference at the National Arts Club was my last-ditch effort to save face.

When my all-star attorney Gloria Allred and I emerged, the room of reporters came alive like an animatronic display. For a moment, I felt as powerful a villain as they'd made me out to be.

Gloria spoke first, calling the whole situation a witch hunt.

"Everyone has a past," Allred said, "and people should be judged for what they do while they are employed, and not for their past sex life."

Cameras and microphones pointed at Gloria, the professional, while I fixed an earnest look on my face. As she talked, I focused on looking normal, or whatever I thought normal looked like in a situation like that.

I believed then—as I do now—that there is nothing morally wrong with working as a prostitute. Women have the right to do with their body what they please, and individuals who work in the sex trades deserve rights and protections. I believed in my right to speak freely about my past and share my opinions, however controversial, and I stood firm in all these convictions.

But the unrelenting humiliation—the *shame*—I felt in that moment had me doubting myself and my beliefs.

When Gloria finished, I stepped over to the mic.

"I have decided to resign as a teacher for the New York City Public School system," my speech began. "It was my belief, as well as that of my attorney, that the First Amendment protected my right to publish my experiences and opinions—however controversial—and that I did not waive my rights by becoming a government employee. The Department of Education, however, disagreed.

"Regardless of the outcome of a trial—which I have every reason to believe I would have won—I do not believe I would have ever been welcomed back to the classroom by the Department of Education, and I have no interest in putting myself in places where I am not welcome."

I looked up to see if anyone could tell that I was lying. The truth was that a team of pro bono lawyers had made it clear that had I brought the case to trial, I almost certainly would have lost. Before this, on day one and within the first fifteen minutes of a hearing between myself and the DOE, the arbitrator told me that I was going to be fired for misconduct, which meant I wouldn't qualify for unemployment. What would I do then? he had asked, lacking the decency to conceal his smirk. I had no savings, no family, no means to support myself. Five months after the scandal first broke, I had no job on the horizon. I was unemployed and unemployable.

I was choosing to surrender my rights and resign rather than see my case to trial in exchange for the promise that the DOE wouldn't contest my claim for unemployment insurance. Without it, I didn't know what I'd have to do to survive, and I was terrified.

With those words, I quit my job in front of the entire New York City press corps. My mortification was complete.

. . . .

Shame is a pernicious emotion that defies definition. It's the painful distress that comes from knowing you've not lived up to an expectation, however unrealistic or impossible that expectation might be. Not only have you failed, but in shame, you hold *yourself* singularly responsible for that failure.

At its core, shame is an existential feeling of unworthiness and profound inadequacy. It is not just the fear that others will find you unlovable. It is a deep-down fear that you don't deserve to be loved.

Shame makes a person feel unique. You feel extraordinary, but it's a painful exceptionalism. In recovery, you'll sometimes hear it described as feeling like "a piece of shit in the center of the universe." That's exactly how it felt the day of the press conference: shame makes us feel as conspicuous and unwanted as a dog turd.

It's the same feeling I experience a decade later when I realize I've forgotten a friend's birthday, I don't have twenty bucks to kick toward the teachers' end-of-year presents, or my kids act up in a public space. The details and severity may change but that chilling, horrific feeling of shame is recognizable to all of us. Especially women.

Like most women, I've spent my lifetime at odds with this painful and largely unspoken human emotion. I've compromised female friendships, walked away from professional opportunities, skipped meals, told lies about myself, my children, and my marriage, and spent countless hours in the gym—all in a desperate attempt to avoid shame. Some days, the slightest embarrassment—or even just the *fear* of embarrassment—turns me into Stephen King's Carrie.

Center stage and covered in pig's blood, I lash out with a primal rage at anyone within my vicinity. Someone will insult me on social media or I'll stumble upon an unflattering photo of myself or I'll feel slighted in some interaction at the store. And instead of softening to the seemingly unbearable fact that I am imperfect or fallible or just not precisely what the world wants me to be, I hear shame whisper, *Dude, what's wrong with you?*

And I explode.

As we'll learn, some people are more inclined to run and hide, hoping to evade shame's mortification. Others freeze or become servile and submissive. Me, I fight. In the two decades since the *New York Post* dubbed me a "prosti-teacher," I continue to wage equally unwinnable battles: against the troll on Twitter that I let get to me, against the other driver I accidentally cut off on the Parkway, against the customer service agent in the unfortunate position of informing me that our insurance won't cover couple's counseling. I resist the inevitable decay of my body by spending money I don't have on yet another antiaging serum or cramming another spin class into my already jam-packed day. Rather than simply apologize for losing my temper, I'll go toe-to-toe with a toddler, turn a neighbor into an enemy, or banish my relatively innocent husband to the couch.

Which, inevitably, leads to more shame. It's a vicious cycle.

My friends rarely use the word "shame," but I feel it in their stories. When we agonize over how to care for our aging parents, begin to talk frankly about our marriages, or admit how we really feel about what happened to our careers once we had kids, shame is often lurking in the corners of our consciousness. Any time we reveal something that puts us at odds with what society expects of us and make ourselves vulnerable to judgment, shame is nearby at the ready to insert itself into the mix.

We call it tough love and tell ourselves it's for our own good, as if believing the lie that we are inadequate will somehow magically assist our bid for self-improvement. Rather than motivating, to me shame is paralyzing. It's the feeling of numbness when I realize I've forgotten a pediatrician's appointment (*What kind of mother neglects to prioritize her children's health?*), or the helplessness when I'm baking a pie for a neighbor and the damn crust doesn't turn out right (*I pride myself on being a good neighbor as well as a good pie maker; now I've ruined both*). Shame is the vulnerability hangover that hits me on the way home from my son's parent-teacher conference, when I find myself replaying every last thing I said (*Why can't I just shut up?*). It's at the root of the resentment I feel toward my husband when I find yesterday's crumbs on the dining room table (*Why doesn't he share my pathological need for everything to be just so?*).

For everyone, but for women especially, shame blocks the paths toward freedom and autonomy, cajoling us into choices that may not serve us in the long run. We leave jobs rather than confront or work alongside our harassers. We remain in romantic relationships that offer little more than financial stability and social standing. We deliver babies "naturally" even when doing so can pose a mortal risk. We stay home rather than breastfeed on a public toilet or pump in a broom closet because we've been convinced that "breast is best."

If we let it, shame will destroy our friendships, erode our romantic relationships, compromise our parenting, and tank our careers. That's why I made it my mission to befriend my foe. I spent the past two decades of my life coming to terms with this most primitive and universal of human emotions, learning my individual shame triggers, and researching shame's impact on others as well as on our culture at large. I couldn't defeat shame, and so I surrendered to it. I invited the unwanted visitor in and I listened patiently to the story it told me about my worth. Only then, having heard it, could I rewrite that story on my own terms.

Shame may be natural, I've learned, but the way it functions in our society is not. The fact that women experience shame more frequently, and more intensely, isn't some biological glitch: it's the direct result of a patriarchal culture that urges women to feel bad about themselves . . . and then punishes us when we do.

Egyptian American journalist and feminist social commentator Mona Eltahawy put it best when she wrote: "Patriarchy deploys shame like a drone: it shadows you, ready to take you out any minute, exhausting you by keeping you forever aware of its presence to the detriment of all other things that you could be investing your attention in."

The incontrovertible truth is that shame has been weaponized against women in particular to prevent us from knowing our value and accomplishing our goals. But it doesn't have to be this way. The cure is telling and claiming our own stories, and that's what you'll do in the course of this book.

. . . .

The methodology of this book is simple: beyond my story, you'll find interviews with hundreds of real women talking about their self-conscious feelings and fears of inadequacy, including some of the most brilliant women of our time. Together, we'll ask and answer the questions: What are we ashamed of? Where is that shame coming from? What are we doing about it?

In part 1, I'll begin to identify the misogynistic roots of our feelings of inadequacy. I'll explain why women experience shame more frequently, and more intensely, than men, and how incessant self-hate influences our behaviors and choices, oftentimes unconsciously.

Then, in part 2, I'll focus on what we do about this. We can eradicate shame no more than we can eliminate any other unpleasant feeling. And since we can't eradicate it—we must face it together. Together, let's learn to be critical of the sexist root causes of shame, curious about how and when shame arises in our individual and collective lives, and compassionate toward ourselves and each other when it happens.

"Shame resilience" is a term created by Brené Brown to describe an ability to notice shame, process it, and then let it go—all without allowing it to change how we view ourselves. According to Brown, this is how we grow through shame rather than allowing it to control us.

By reaching out and sharing our personal stories, however shameful, we develop a clearer sense of who we are and what we believe. And we create a world where others are equally emboldened to express who they are, understand how they feel, and ask for what they need.

Rather than allowing ourselves to just *be*, shame makes it so that we are constantly striving to be more, be better, be *different*. So it's ironic that when I am aware of my shame, I am in closer contact with my personal ideals. It is paradoxical, but when I acknowledge (rather than ignore or avoid) shame, I am a better wife, mother, friend, and feminist.

A word on that word, "feminist." The fact that this book centers itself around the experiences of women and other gender minorities makes it, by definition, feminist. The strategies for healing from shame are, similarly, feminist actions: telling our stories, returning to the body, feeling our truths, and developing critical awareness. Sitting in groups, large and small, and learning to listen to ourselves and each other with empathy and compassion—these are feminist acts. Simply put: sisterhood can help us acknowledge our inner demons and where they come from, seize control of what is in our power, and transform shame into compassion. It isn't about "fighting" shame because when you fight a feeling, you're at war with yourself. Instead, freedom comes from getting quiet and curious, and welcoming and accepting the feeling so as to allow it to pass. Only then can you turn to fight the *real* enemy: the institutions weaponizing our perfectly natural emotions against us.

At the same time that this is an unapologetically feminist work, this book will also critique the role shame has had in the feminist movement. We'll examine how shame has played a part in the way society and the mainstream feminist movement have historically silenced certain female experiences and whole categories of people. We're told that there's a "right" way to be a woman—even a liberated, modern woman—and if we stray too far out of those lines, shame is a tool to drive us back in. I want to give voice to the acute pain this erasure has caused in my life, as well as the lives of those I love, including but not limited to sex workers.

With that, I want to share a definition of "woman" by Monica Hesse, columnist for the *Washington Post*. As Hesse wrote for the *Washington Post* in 2022, "The act of being a woman often has less to do with biology than it has to do with how you move through the world and what you see and worry about on the way." Womanhood, Hesse maintains, relates to "how people treat you. The respect you are afforded or denied. The knowledge you are assumed to have or lack. The laws that are permitted to regulate the most intimate parts of your body.

"To some people," Hesse writes, "the definition of being a woman may feel immutable and fixed, limited only to genetic makeup or the reproductive organs we have at birth. Others of us are reminded of our womanhood when we step out into the world each day and offer ourselves for judgment." When I talk about "women," this is who and what I'm talking about. If you identify as a woman, I'm talking about you.

Just as women everywhere struggle to connect to ourselves and our emotional experience, we struggle to connect with other women—particularly those with experiences we deem dissimilar to our own. Shame isolates us, and it isolates others. This is why it is so deadly.

I mean that literally. Rafts of studies show that shame has an insidious, pervasive, and pernicious influence on our health. Shame is closely linked with a wide range of psychological difficulties—depression, psychosis, post-traumatic stress disorder, eating disorders, and other conditions associated with a shorter life expectancy.

Whatever its trigger, shame keeps us silent and silence keeps us from receiving support. Fearful of rejection, we don't disclose a truth that might elicit a kind word from a friend, let alone medical advice from a doctor. Shame can get in the way of a patient seeking treatment and it can keep us from disclosing the full details of our physical and mental health to our doctor, which may result in inadequate or ineffective treatment being prescribed. It can also lower treatment adherence, meaning that we're less likely to follow doctors' orders.

And shame itself is bad for our health. A team of researchers at the Cardiovascular Stress Response Lab at the School of Kinesiology and Health Studies of Queen's University found shame temporarily decreased artery function, leading them to speculate that people who frequently experience a lot of shame may have an increased risk of developing cardiovascular disease. A separate 2022 study titled "Racism, Shame, and Stress Reactivity" found that Black women who experienced high levels of shame during the past year and over their lifetime—including "shame related to frequent racist experiences"—demonstrated even greater cortisol reactivity, the stress hormone that can increase cholesterol, triglycerides, blood sugar levels, and blood pressure. These are all common risk factors of heart disease, the leading cause of death for women in the United States.

It's no exaggeration to say that shame is literally killing us.

Beyond shame's impact on our physical health, there is its more insidious impact: the self-annihilation we risk when we reject the parts of ourselves we might cherish if not for shame. I have denied, cut off, and abandoned aspects of myself for fear that others couldn't or wouldn't accept me as I truly was. And the painful reality is that I haven't always been accepted. The loss of my career as a public-school teacher is just one vivid example of how I have been made to feel anomalous. But I am not unique, and neither are you.

Whatever your shame, we've all been there. We all know that feeling. These days, when I find myself in this utterly forsaken place, I know just what to do. I know that shame is an opportunity to come back to reality, to revise my thinking about myself and the world, and to realize a deeper truth. Just as soon as I recognize the feeling of shame crawling up my spine, I steady myself. Instead of squashing it down, or running away, I allow the feeling to be. At first blush, I get quiet and really, *really* curious. I stand outside the feeling and examine it with the same intense attention a small kid gives a bug. My son, Oscar, can spend hours with an insect, even a frightening one. He is cautious, wary, until slowly but steadily he realizes the nature of the beast, be it a butterfly or a dung beetle. Whatever its nature, he and the relatively harmless creature can coexist. Even if it stings, he trusts that he can keep himself safe.

Yes, a feeling as intense as shame can be terrifying. But we can do this, too.

We can pay close attention to something that scares us.

Part 1

Identifying Shame

1

Perfect Monsters

How Society Weaponizes Shame Against Women

My neighbor Penny tells me that she hits herself. A fortysomething-year-old, happily married stay-at-home mom to one exceptionally well-behaved toddler, she's not exactly the person you'd picture pounding her own fists into her head. Penny's the kind of woman who still irons her husband's shirts, a middle-class white lady living in the suburbs who deadheads petunias and handwrites thank-you cards. Penny's the woman in your friend group who makes the reservation. When there's a shitty job no one wants to do, she's the mom who happily volunteers first.

Self-harm isn't exactly what most consider normal, yet the gist of what started Penny's undoing will sound familiar to every woman everywhere: by her own account, Penny piles too much on her plate, then feels ashamed because she can't get it all done while the stress of trying to do so, she says, makes her act like "a monster."

It happened just this past Saturday, Penny told me, when she and her family were leaving for a weekend trip to the beach. Her husband, Greg, stood at the door, keys in hand, while Penny rushed around the house, packing and tidying, getting angrier by the minute until Greg expressed gentle impatience, and Penny's rage boiled over. She shouted at her husband, who—Penny said—just stood there, momentarily dumbfounded, before he started shouting back in defense.

"And now Greg and I are shouting at each other, and Hudson is crying, and then everyone is crying." Until, Penny said, she resorted to an old coping mechanism as a way of making it stop: "I went into the bathroom, locked the door, sat on the toilet, and started hitting myself in the head."

Penny's casual laughter belied the struggle to trust me and find the courage to be real. I held eye contact as she said it even as my pulse quickened. In our culture, we're conditioned to find another's shame entertaining, and I'm no exception. But I am aware this is a problem, and so rather than feel titillated by my friend's pain, I found ways to empathize. When Penny described her growing anxiety behind the urgent need to make the beds, to replace damp towels with dry ones, to quickly make and pack yet another snack, I could relate to my friend's perfectionism. I, too, have felt the frantic fear that I was forgetting something, the compulsive need to wash every last dish in the sink.

Still, I struggled to synthesize this new information with what I thought I knew about Penny. Of all the moms in our friend group, Penny and Greg appear to have the strongest marriage. They probably have the most money. Hudson's always the best behaved. Penny's the friend who never loses her patience.

She's the mom who always remembers to pack snacks.

Penny never used the word "shame" but I felt it as she told me her story. It pulsed quietly as she described paralyzing anxiety and self-hatred. Even as she shrugged it off casually and softened it with humor, I felt her pain.

Most of us have heard the term "shame spiral," coined by clinical psychologist Gershen Kaufman to describe the loss of control triggered by an unsettling event.

That's what happened that day to Penny: failing to live up to society's outdated yet persistent image of the perfect wife and mother, Penny lashed out at her husband, which only made the feeling worse. Even as she felt angry with Greg for not being more helpful, she ultimately blamed herself and took responsibility for the whole situation—so much so that she felt deserving of punishment, which she then inflicted on herself behind the closed bathroom door.

Penny's not only a neighbor, she's also a close friend. Still, it's not unusual for people I barely know to tell me equally personal things. Benign conversations with relative strangers naturally gravitate toward the edges of the permissible. While those around us engage in polite conversation, we're exchanging stories about blow jobs we gave strangers in our twenties or all those extremely regrettable times we lost our shit on our kid.

I tell myself that it's because as a journalist, I'm trained to ask just the right questions. But I know it happens more frequently when people are aware of my own complicated past. These confidantes know that I have experiences in the sex industry, that I was publicly shamed for writing and speaking about these experiences in 2010, and that I still frequently write and speak publicly about these and other presumably shameful experiences.

It happens so often that I sometimes refer to myself as the "shame whisperer."

Whatever the cause, I seem to have a unique, even uncanny ability to Dr. Pimple Pop the darkest secrets out of people. And based on the number of confidences that I receive, this sort of unloading seems to be exactly what a lot of folks long for.

Don't get me wrong: most people would do everything in their power to avoid judgment, let alone humiliation. When we don't measure up to society's expectations of us, we feel deeply flawed and alone. These are intensely painful feelings. No one wants to feel shame.

At the same time, from my unique vantage point, I really do suspect most folks crave a less filtered life. How wonderful it would be if we could speak openly about our messiness, neither glamorizing it nor minimizing our pain. We'd all rather *not* hide aspects of ourselves and our experiences out of a fear of rejection. We'd all rather be completely ourselves, entirely honest and at ease, and still feel as if we belong. We all want to live unafraid to share who we *really* are and what's *really* on our mind. We all want to be the same person regardless of the audience—to have integrity, in spite of our fear. We are as desperate to embody our truths as we are terrified to do so.

So what's stopping us?

What Is Shame, Really?

Shame is a pernicious emotion, one that evades recognition even as it permeates every aspect of our lives. Defined most simply, it's the painful distress that comes from believing we haven't lived up to an expectation: When there is something we think we should have done or been or said or did—but didn't or weren't—shame takes hold. It doesn't matter if the expectation was realistic or impossible. *I failed,* we think, *and it's my fault.*

I asked my Facebook friends to describe how it felt, the last time they were struck by shame. Unsurprisingly, a lot of people misinterpreted the assignment. Instead of focusing on themselves, the majority of responders reflected the question outward: offering definitions, referring me to experts, recommending books. If they shared a personal shame story, they told me the details of what happened rather than how it had made them *feel*.

The fact that folks struggled to describe the physiological response in their bodies is unsurprising; we are not a culture accustomed to describing our feelings. Shame, in particular, defies words. This is because, as we are feeling it, shame seizes our limbic system while shutting down the parts of our brain that are capable of language.

Still, a handful of people answered the question the way I was hoping they would. My friend from high school, Al, described shame as a feeling of intense embarrassment, sadness, and regret.

"I have many memories that I look back on that make me physically ill," he said. "A lot of the time I'm intensely critical of myself after feeling shame, too, and that always turns into depression, even suicidal thoughts in the past."

"Physically, it starts with prickly heat on top of my head, neck, shoulders, back, and arms," Heather said. "Then my vision gets really clear but my hearing seems diminished, and my heart rate increases. Then there's the replay on a loop of whatever it is I'm ashamed of."

"It's more than feeling uncomfortable," Patty Ann said. "It makes me not want to exist."

As with any feeling, what triggers shame differs from person to person. Whereas just the thought of trying on bathing suits might spark extreme anxiety and body hatred in some people, the same situation might elicit a more subtle or even an entirely different emotional response in someone else.

Odds are, though, that you find bathing suit shopping at least a little bit triggering. It's so ubiquitous a trigger that it's been studied: in 2012, researchers at Flinders University in Australia found that just imagining ourselves in a dressing room trying on swimsuits will put most women in a bad mood.

Appearance and body image, family and parenting. Money and work. Mental and physical health. Addiction. Sex. Aging. The traumas we survived. The stereotypes we endure. These are the things, according to social scientists, that really set off our shame reflex.

We are set off, or "triggered," whenever we fear we have failed to meet society's expectations of who, how, and what we should be. In her foundational book *Women and Shame*, American professor and writer Brené Brown makes clear how we pick up on these expectations from our family and friends (teachers, mentors, health professionals, work colleagues, faith communities, neighbors), as well as from the media (books, music, magazines, movies and television, and the advertising that permeates all facets of modern life). The messages of what we "should be" are so complex and competing that they're frequently unattainable . . . and yet, we internalize them and develop what psychologists call "negative self-talk." In some cases, negative self-talk sounds like "I'm so stupid." Usually, it's more subtle. Maybe when you tell yourself "I shouldn't have done that," the "I'm so stupid" stays silent—but it's there.

Shame is frequently confused for other self-conscious emotions.

- **Embarrassment**, for example, also arises when we become aware that we've broken social norms. The difference is that when we feel embarrassed, we will often, eventually, be able to see the humor in the situation. In some instances, we may deflect shame with humor, but we don't really find it funny; in fact, it is incredibly difficult to speak of. Embarrassment can bring folks together, whereas unprocessed shame does the opposite: it

disconnects us from others, and from ourselves, because we feel
the need to hide whatever we're ashamed of at all costs.

- Shame is more similar to **humiliation**, in that both feelings are
incredibly painful and long-lasting. Take embarrassment and
elongate its half-life tenfold. The difference between shame and
humiliation is that we recognize a humiliation as undeserved,
whereas when in shame, we believe the mistreatment we're
enduring is our fault.

- Shame is most frequently confused with **guilt**—the *I shouldn't
have done that* feeling when you make a mistake or do
something wrong. The difference? Guilt can motivate a person
to change a behavior, make amends, apologize, or rethink our
priorities, whereas shame does none of these things. Shame shuts
us down, and we are unlikely to take positive actions to address
our misdeeds because we don't see our behaviors as the problem;
we see *ourselves* and our whole being as fundamentally flawed.
Shame is less a feeling that you've done something bad than it is
a feeling that you *are* bad.

If you're not sure of shame's impact on you and your life, it might
help to listen to the stories of other women probably a lot like yourself. I interviewed 150-plus women and gender nonconforming/non-
binary folks, plus some cisgender men, on the topic near (if not dear)
to all of our hearts. Together, we explored all the ways that shame is
weaponized against women to prevent us from knowing our worth
and achieving our goals. We talked about the "big" shames we carry,
but also those everyday moments where we feel unnecessarily cruddy
about ourselves because we're just not meeting some (usually impossible) expectation.

The following quotes illustrate just how endemic shame is to our everyday experience:

Now that I am a mother, there is even more pressure to be selfless, always putting my child's needs before my own. Ever since I was young, I have struggled with self-worth.

In my culture, mental health is just not talked about. There's a phrase in Chinese that translates to mean "eat bitter," meaning suffering is part of life. My dad would say this phrase to me. You just have to work hard, and not complain. My ADD went undiagnosed, and I struggled.

An old boss of mine . . . would call me at 4:00 a.m. stressed, would only reach out to me when I made a mistake, and would make comments on calls with others that I wasn't wearing makeup. I would work seventy to eighty hours a week for him almost to "prove him wrong," only to be met with shame at the end of every day.

Sex is complicated for me because of my history. There are things that have happened to me that make intimacy on any level really hard.

I present as straight. I have only been in heterosexual relationships. I think that my family would quickly write me off as attention seeking if I ever defined myself outside of the way that they see me, which is difficult because they don't even really know me.

For a long time, I didn't feel comfortable in my body, and to be honest, after giving birth I still struggle with this a bit. I'm embarrassed by my flabby stomach that won't go away. I am ashamed of feeling this way.

Now that I am an "older woman," I'm always looking at younger women mournfully . . . I look at almost everyone I see and feel like I failed.

Still the Issue of the Day

Twenty years ago, Brené Brown called shame a "silent epidemic." In *Women and Shame*, Brown identified the emotion as being at the root of a whole host of personal struggles and social ills, including depression, anxiety, eating disorders, and addiction. Her work lays clear how these and other problems are the natural consequences of what she deems our "culture of shame"—a society that does not allow most of us, but women in particular, to make missteps or mistakes.

It was a message that resonated. Brené Brown went on to achieve true guru status with her TED Talk on the topic, which has received more than ten million views and literally hundreds of glowing-with-gratitude comments. Women were delirious with relief to have shame named for them, and to be offered reassuring kindness, relatable antidotes, and practical advice on how to ease our very real, individual pain.

From Brown's success sprung a whole movement of anti-shame experts who launched an all-out war on shame. Glennon Doyle has written multiple books riffing on the theme that we are born to be warriors, and discussing how we can individually find the strength, bravery, and power to battle shame. Author and yoga instructor Jennifer Pastiloff hosts "shame loss" workshops, seminars, events, and retreats where women work to free themselves from the shackles of shame by embracing their inner asshole and ceasing to give a fuck. And there are many more.

The anti-shame movement has shone a light on the pain that comes with constantly fearing and focusing on one's perceived inadequacies. And yet, shame remains no less pervasive today than it was ten, twenty, or even thirty years ago. We spend $192.2 billion and $511 billion respectively on diet culture and the beauty industry; still, one in five adults feel ashamed of their bodies. When you focus just on teenage girls, that number soars to seven in ten. Women earn more college and graduate degrees than men and we make up more than half the workforce—yet research finds that girls and women remain woefully less self-assured compared to men. More than 75 percent of executive women suffer from imposter syndrome. Among working women with children, only one in four feel they are effectively balancing motherhood and their careers.

We've come a long way toward giving women the freedom and dignity to live full lives, with jobs and ambitions and self-directed choice. So why aren't we feeling good about ourselves? Why has our culture of shame only gotten worse?

One of the reasons shame still persists is because some people, including some experts, think it can be useful. Some developmental psychologists argue that there is such a thing as "positive" shame, and that a mild feeling of self-censure helps children regulate their behavior and follow the rules. In his book *Shame: Free Yourself, Find Joy, and Build True Self-Esteem*, psychotherapist Joseph Burgo describes shame as a necessary means of society expressing its values and enforcing expectations of how we ought to behave. Shame promotes social cohesion, he and other experts say, and encourages members of a tribe to obey the rules for a common good.

Shame may "work" in the sense that it will elicit a behavior change in the short term, but it isn't an effective strategy for producing *meaningful* changes in behavior—and, according to researchers, it can actually end up causing more harm than good. Rafts of studies demonstrate that childhood shame leads to chronic anxiety, low self-esteem, feelings of emptiness, perfectionism, unhealthy relationships, and a lack of healthy self-love. Similarly, research finds that adults who are prone to shame are more susceptible to psychological problems including depression and anxiety. Rather than promoting social cohesion, shame *reduces* an adult's tendency to behave in socially constructive ways.

Shame won't result in meaningful, long-lasting behavioral change—but assuming it did, let's look more closely at just what values our society tries to shame us into sharing. What, exactly, do those in power consider "socially constructive"? It's generally not abusive men or corrupt politicians who are hanging their heads and blushing with contrition; it's the woman who can't keep up with her family's dirty laundry or the waitress after a customer slips his hand up her skirt. It's not the CEO caught cheating on his pregnant wife with the intern who is shamed; it's the intern who loses professional opportunities. Or it's the pregnant wife who gets shunned by her neighbors and loses friends. No, all that shame is not positive, nor is it accidental.

When you recognize that shame is primarily piled on top of women, girls, and other marginalized groups, it becomes pretty unconscionable to argue this pattern is somehow socially beneficial. The emotion may be natural, but there's nothing natural about the way it operates in our world. Shame persists in spite of all our best efforts against it because, in a misogynistic culture, that is what it's designed to do. Shame is weaponized to serve its (sexist) goal. And women everywhere are sick of it.

What's Race Got to Do With It?

Is it enough to think only about "women and shame"? Certainly not. Each of us brings our own unique background of experience, perspective, and—yes—identity to the topic. And it's important to acknowledge the differences so that we can also find the commonalities among our stories.

Even before the scholar Kimberlé Crenshaw introduced the term "intersectionality" and it became a buzzword, feminists like Patricia Hill Collins, Angela Davis, and bell hooks challenged the notion that gender was the primary factor determining a woman's fate (and you can go all the way back to Sojourner Truth's *Ain't I a Woman?*). Black feminist scholarship has called out a feminist movement led by and premised on white, middle-class women's experiences, and its false suggestion of homogeneity among all women based on those women's experiences.

Simply put, not all women's experiences—including our experiences with shame—are the same.

Crenshaw, for example, called out the assumption that men are taught to be powerful, women are assumed to be passive—something I heard occasionally in the interviews I conducted—reminding readers that this is not necessarily true of the Black experience.

Rather than seeing Black women as overly emotional and in need of protection, society assumes they are resilient, independent, and emotionally restrained—so strong as to be indestructible. This perceived indestructibility of Black women "has long been an excuse for overwork and underprotection, a rationalization for our exploitation and abuse that has morphed into a dangerous stereotype that we have all too often internalized," Crenshaw says in a 2017 report entitled "Leading from the Black: How Black Women Lead Even When Ignored."

What a trick: weaponizing a woman's own strength against herself. It is one of countless examples of how women can't escape criticism and that, when it comes to shame and how it functions in our society, it's really damned if you do, damned if you don't.

The fact that Black and other POC women's experiences with shame were markedly different from white women's encounters revealed itself in my interviews. You'll hear white women struggle with how pop culture portrayals obscure their own authentic lived experiences, but when I talked with Nkenge, who is Black and queer, she explained that her experience was different: "I don't find myself comparing myself to others often. That is a benefit of being a lesbian Muslim, I guess. We are not an especially visible group, so I don't even know what we're supposed to look like or how we're expected to behave."

Instead, Nkenge described feeling "the pressure of being palatable enough for white, straight, conservative consumption," and the shame that came from the feeling of sometimes falling short. She also described a pressure to be exceptional, "so that my being smart and productive cancels out my being a woman, a Black person, a gay person."

This was echoed by nearly every woman from an immigrant/minority group who I interviewed—the need to be a "model minority" and differentiate oneself from the disreputable category, and the pressure to work twice as hard to be respectable.

"I don't see myself from a singular lens, 'just woman' or 'just wife,'" Shabana said. "My identity as a brown woman impacts how I am seen and treated. As a result, it affects how I show up in the world."

Beyond the need for inclusivity, understanding how Black women and other minorities experience shame unlocks important truths about the emotion and how it operates in our world. Namely, shame and shaming are bound up with social inequality and how it reflects and serves to reinforce, reinstate, and legitimize a white, middle-class, heteronormative patriarchal status quo. Academics like Tamara Shefer and many others have been exploring these ideas for years. This is why women and other gender minorities, as well as people of color, more than cisgender men, are shamed and shunned.

Another reason I suspect we haven't gotten a grip on shame is because it's true that a lot of anti-shame experts don't talk enough about politics. In the beginning, even Brené Brown made a point to describe shame as neither a Red state nor Blue state issue and kept her politics largely to herself, arguing that while she may have a political identity, her work did not. But by 2016, Brown defied her nonpartisan approach and expressed outrage over the news that then-presidential candidate Donald Trump had repeatedly made vulgar comments about women to television personality Billy Bush of *Access Hollywood*.

"Let's be clear," Brown wrote on Instagram. "Calling this 'guy talk' is an insult to all of the good men and boys out there." On

Twitter she added to the sentiment: "This is what rape culture looks like and sounds like." But in response to her words, some fans expressed disappointment, frustration, and even rage. The most common response she received, Brown later shared on her website, was, "Stick to research and making people feel better."

"If you're wondering if I believe that the left has the corner on the wholehearted market, the answer is no. The work is apolitical," Brown maintained in that same website post. "I will say, however, that I've never seen anyone in my lifetime—Republican, Democrat, or Independent—who has leveraged fear, shame, and dehumanization to divide our country like Donald Trump has." In the years since, Brené Brown has stuck her neck out not just for women but for Black people, Indigenous people, people with disabilities, trans people, immigrants, Muslims, poor people—the list goes on. And she's collaborated with other voices, amplifying Black women in particular. She and Tarana Burke co-edited *You Are Your Best Thing*, an anthology featuring Black writers sharing their experiences with shame and vulnerability. Of course, people of color had been doing the work long before Brené Brown came along and sparked an anti-shame movement. At its best, and at its root, shame resilience has always been intersectional—a radical, transgressive, and profoundly political act.

Learning to Listen to Pain

For as long as I have been paying attention, women have been rising up defiantly against shame. In the late 1960s, "the personal is political" became a rallying cry. Ever since Betty Friedan published *The Feminine Mystique* in 1963, women with children have openly discussed the less-flattering aspects of motherhood. In the last de-cade in particular, we've entered a new era of women going public to make sense of complicated sexual experiences. Well before I found my voice, sex workers were bravely stepping out of the shadows, fighting legislation that criminalizes their industry by offering their honest accounts of how bad laws further complicate their already difficult lives. Thanks to the #MeToo movement, we're talking more as a culture about sexual harassment and "bad sex" in even broader terms, and conceding that, when it comes to healthy sexuality, con-sent is not enough.

Still, even within this fight, even the best of us struggle to connect to our emotional experience.

As my friend the author Ashley C. Ford once put it in a group chat, "My thinking self knows that there are no feelings you aren't allowed to feel. My feeling self is still catching up to that."

In this particular conversation, someone was venting about par-enting, and the shame they felt for being anything less than patient with their insolent stepkid.

"I don't begrudge any of you the huge job of raising angry teens, but I wish I had been allowed to be angry back then," Ashley said. "I was in my mid-thirties before I could get mad without feeling like the feeling itself made me a bad person."

Ashley is the author of the *New York Times* best-selling memoir *Somebody's Daughter*. She's written everywhere on the topics of race, sexuality, and body image. And still she struggles to understand and respect her emotional experience.

As she puts it, "Every once in a while I discover something new I'm allowed to be mad about."

When Ashley said this, I could definitely relate. I've never had a problem expressing anger—if anything, it's been an emotional go-to for me. But for most of my twenties, I hid my softer feelings, including shame, even from myself—thinking they couldn't hurt me if I refused to acknowledge them. Even now, it is sometimes tempting to think I can reason away an uncomfortable feeling. If I just keep googling, I will read the right article and educate myself straight out of the grips of shame. And yes, education is a part of shame resilience—but it's only one part of it.

This attitude that shame is the bad guy, and that it can be overcome if only I fight hard enough, is learned. Women of my generation were taught to rage against rape culture, and reclaim slurs like "slut," "bitch," and "whore." In college, I became "sex positive," and rose up against body shaming, fat shaming, mommy shaming, the list went on. Before many of us found ourselves in a traditional marriage, we brazenly mocked heterosexist norms.

By the mid-2000s, women all over the internet were defiantly confessing our most personal stories as a way of expunging ourselves of the painful . . . or skipping this step altogether and defiantly refusing to feel shame. After I lost my career as a schoolteacher and became a freelance writer, I joined this army of self-identified feminists, who by then were waging an all-out war against the emotion. For a while there, it really felt as if shamelessness had become the ultimate #girlboss act. But that bravado could only take us so far.

For most of my life, I have intellectualized shame to take control of it. But an important fact about shame—and any emotion—is that we feel it even when we think we ought to know better. Take, for example, when I was in the first trimester of my first pregnancy and my OB started lecturing me about my weight gain, casually suggesting I "lay off the carbs." I knew on an intellectual level that what she was saying was wrong. I knew with all the brain in my skull that I was a perfectly healthy weight, and even if I had been overweight by medical standards, I knew that it was perfectly normal and typically healthy to gain weight when you are pregnant, and that, in fact, it is perfectly healthy to be what our society deems "overweight."

And still, that day my face grew hot, and I sputtered some weak defense about morning sickness and uncontrollable cravings. I walked out of the office furious at a world seemingly hell-bent on undermining women's power and happiness even as, simultaneously, my mind started down the rabbit hole of how I was going to control my eating. Underneath my anger and against all reason, I felt ashamed.

The shame didn't help me lose any weight, by the way. It rarely does.

"Shame is the deepest of the 'negative emotions,' a feeling we will do almost anything to avoid," writes Gabor Maté in *When the Body Says No: The Cost of Hidden Stress*. "Unfortunately, our abiding fear of shame impairs our ability to see reality."

Maté is a Holocaust survivor and physician who became a renowned expert on trauma, addiction, and stress. He and other experts on the biopsychosocial aspects of pathology make clear how unfelt emotions can burble up in surprising and unpleasant ways. Sometimes shame can metastasize into depression. You feel like a phony, and you act in ways that are discordant with your beliefs. Sometimes shame will transmute into anger, which is rarely good for your relationships or your sense of self. Or shame might take the form of silence, allowing a small problem to balloon into a larger, unwieldy predicament.

As Maté puts it, "The attempt to escape from pain, is what creates more pain." Relief begins when you let down your guard, return to your body, and let yourself feel the emotion you're trying so fervently to avoid. Do this and you're likely to discover the source of your emotional pain isn't actually some sort of inherent worthlessness—that it is, instead, some sexist cultural expectation you've mistaken for your own belief.

Speaking Truth to Shame

A decade since the loss of my career in elementary education, I'm a successful freelance writer, wife, and mom of two. I am incredibly shame resilient. Still, no one is immune. At this very moment, shame is nagging at me, telling me I ought to be spending this time with my family. Never mind that I feel equally guilty when I'm with them, ashamed that I'm neglecting my career. Shame is how I feel when my preschooler wants me to build LEGO boats but I'd rather be working, trawling Facebook Marketplace, unloading the dishwasher, doing basically anything but focusing my undivided attention on the interests of a three-year-old child. Shame explains why my husband's every gentle suggestion feels like the sharpest of criticisms. Why I snap when he asks if the kids have sunscreen on, and then I feel ashamed for snapping, fearing that a better wife wouldn't speak to her husband like that.

As an individual, I accept that I am no match for the institutions that target me. I still have days where I'm crying in the shower, overwhelmed with exhaustion because the challenges of marriage and motherhood are relentless, but I can't complain because I ought to enjoy it. After all, *the days are long, but the years are short* and *it goes by so fast.*

Slogans like these are often offered in comfort, but until women are given permission to express our messy realities and the nuanced feelings that come with them, platitudes only further our anxiety. A mug emblazoned with some defiant slogan is no substitute for political rights. Moms don't want sentimentality, bunches of flowers, and brunch one day a year. We want legislative victories that protect our rights and afford us more freedoms. Whatever our experience, we need unfiltered commiseration with folks in the same trenches and practical strategies for surviving hard years.

None of this is possible so long as we stay silent.

This takes me back to that moment with Penny, when she confessed to hitting herself in the bathroom out of frustration. Out of shame. From that day forward, I saw my friend differently. Not negatively, in the way that shame would have us fear, but the opposite: I saw her with a new respect and empathy. I saw myself, too, and all the parts of myself I hide and deny. I recognized those parts of me . . . and I recognized their worth.

Honestly, I live for these moments. Moments when my friends and I transform shame into love and compassion. When we don't, the damage it does to our relationships and to ourselves is incalculable. If we let it, shame will damage our friendships, destroy our romantic relationships, interfere with our parenting, and derail our careers. It will undermine the very things that are most valuable to us. Shame makes us beat ourselves up, sometimes literally. Acknowledging the feeling is where we begin, but it is only a beginning. Telling ourselves and each other "just don't feel that way" isn't enough. We need to do more. And we need to do it together.

There's a popular Buddhist teaching that says when you run after your thoughts, you are like a dog chasing a stick, running after it every time it is thrown. As a society, we are doggedly focused on running after shame. Instead, the teaching goes, we need to be like a lion.

Rather than chasing after shame, we need to turn to face who (or what) threw it.

2

Maybe She's Born with It

Where Shame Begins

We all feel shame. Let me repeat: we all feel shame. The fact that I feel shame, a lot, makes me in no way unique. I remind myself of this as I begin my story. That I still feel shame, and readily admit it, doesn't undermine my authority on the subject. I don't have to be any tougher than I actually am to be taken seriously. And actually, vulnerability is strength.

Sure, I have strategies for dealing with shame and other difficult emotions, but I haven't "overcome" anything. I still experience shame. More than I want to admit. But I do admit it. I admit it because I know what happens when we don't.

Not wanting to feel shame takes me out of my body. It makes me give away my power. It makes me give my power away to men. It makes me give my power away to men who devalue me. The more I am devalued, the more I fight for them to see and recognize my worth. This is a losing strategy, but I still do it.

I *still* do it.

I still leave my body when something is happening to me that I don't like.

In an effort to evade shame, I still act in ways that are discordant with my beliefs. I still do it. We all do, because we've been doing it for a long, long time.

....

I was just fourteen years old when I met Charlie at the Dairy Queen where I worked after high school. Sandy brown hair tucked under a beat-up baseball cap, he wore a Grateful Dead shirt and what qualified as skater shoes. *Just my type,* I thought, as if I were particular.

When he ordered his Blizzard, I noticed an accent and dared to ask where he was from. Iowa, Charlie told me, where he'd gotten himself into trouble.

"Staying the summer at my gram's." He pointed to a white house across the street.

I watched Charlie sit on the curb, eating his Blizzard. He noticed me watching. I coyly looked away. When he finished, he came back to the window, grabbed a napkin, and asked to borrow a pen.

Later that night, I dialed the number. His voice deep and indifferent, he asked if I wanted to go to the movies.

We didn't go to the movies. I told myself at the time that neither of us had really wanted to. Instead, we drove around the streets I'd wandered by foot as a girl.

Do you remember what it was like to be a girl, and those moments when girlhood was becoming something you were desperate to shake off, like how a butterfly must feel when they are breaking free from their cocoon, if butterflies are somehow embarrassed by the fact that they used to look like worms?

This was how I felt then, in that moment, with a boy I barely knew.

Charlie and I drove around until we ended up in the Glens, which is exactly what you'd assume it was, and where, predictably, we started to kiss.

In the woods, he pushed his mouth into mine and pulled off my shirt. He pushed up my bra, exposing my breasts. My bare back pushed against the rough bark of a tree. It became something other than exciting. It was moving too fast. I pushed him firmly on his chest and he stepped back, twigs snapping beneath his sneakers.

"What's wrong?" His voice cracked.

"Nothing."

"You scared?"

"A little."

"Don't be scared," he said.

He took my hands and gently laid me down in the dirt. For a second, he was gone. Then, I felt him kissing me through my cotton underwear. His mouth felt warm and humid, like a classroom the first and last weeks of school.

"Charlie," I said. "You can't. I have my period."

He paused, considering this for a moment.

"You're lying," he said finally, softly. "Relax."

I leaned back as he started again, losing myself to the canopy of trees above me. The atmosphere was heavy, electric. I looked down at my stomach, white blue, and the top of Charlie's head. The sky behind him brightened with a flash of lightning.

"It's going to rain!" I squealed.

"That's only heat lightning," Charlie said.

"Relax," he repeated, tugging off my underwear. The cool night air tickled. Then everything felt hot again, and wet.

I was not in my body in this moment. I was in the trees. I was in the humid classroom, a hostile space where I never felt safe. A space where most are not allowed to be vulnerable. I was too plain, too bookish; I tried too hard and most kids could tell. I was in my confusion, ambivalent over what was happening to my body. It was happening to me, but I was not in control. I wasn't safe, not necessarily. I didn't know this person or what he thought of me. I didn't know what he was capable of or what he might do next.

We didn't have sex that day, or ever. He went down on me and then it was over. I wouldn't have described the experience as anything other than consensual. After it was over, he drove me home. It stormed all night. Lying awake in my bed, I listened to the rain, a new emotion emerging in my chest.

Where Shame Begins

Before shame, Freud says, childhood is a paradise. Then a peculiar and uncomfortable emotion appears. Freud describes shame as an anxiety, an impending sense of harm. He theorized that shame propagates in the space between the ego (that is, who you think you are) and the superego (who you want to be according to society's standards). The loss of bearings and resultant ruminative cognitions, he says, is due to an ineffective caregiver, who—according to early psychoanalysis—is usually the mother. (Shame on you, Mom!)

Shame is a natural part of individuation. As a child learns to feed and clothe themselves, they are separating from the person they've always relied on. Every self-directed action is a move toward autonomy, but we notice our separateness most acutely when we step outside of society's rules. When our mother yanks us back onto the sidewalk, we become aware of our individuality and the power we hold. Shame individuates, but it is a painful individuality. What are *you* doing? Where are *you* going? Look at *you*! What have *you* done?

When a person feels shame, the brain reacts as if facing a physical danger. The prefrontal cortex activates and triggers a cascade of stress hormones, just as it would in response to a physical threat. Our heart beats faster, and we may feel the impulse to run or fight even as the nervous system slams the brakes. We may freeze, turn our eyes away as if hiding, and experience a heavy, sinking feeling in our chest.

We react as if we are being threatened because, in some sense, we are. As children, we are completely dependent on our caregivers, but even as adults, we need others to help us meet our physical and psychological needs. Shame—a fear of rejection—threatens us on a primitive level.

Shame is a natural emotion. It's also a by-product of our cultural background and the values we absorb growing up. When parents punish, friends pressure, the doctor warns, or a teacher rewards, we get the message of who, what, and how we're supposed to be. These messages are organized by gender, shame experts say—what is expected of us as girls and women, or as boys and men.

Like all girls, I learned the rules early, and for the most part I followed them: Be good. Be sweet. Be flirty, but not too flirty. Be sexy, but don't be a slut. Don't be fat, or too thin. Go to the gym and work out, but don't get "bulky." Shave your body. Cover your blemishes. Cover your body, but don't be a prude. Smile more. Be cool. Reflect men's interests, but remain feminine. Go along with what men say, no matter how demeaning. Be assertive, just don't be a bitch. Speak up, lean in. Be demure. You're not hungry, you'll just have a salad. Deny your appetite. Suppress your needs. Deny yourself the sexual pleasure men take for granted. Make yourself just sexually available enough until motherhood when you become invisible. You were just a container all along. Before this, we're told that our body is a temple, a thing of value. A woman's body, we're taught, is a source of power and capital even as we're warned we ought to never take advantage of that. To do so—that is, to trade sex for money—is literally a crime.

When I asked women about what shameful (or shame-inducing) messages they internalized, I heard a multitude of perspectives:

Society wants us to be this perfect human being: full-time mom, full-time wife, superhero. Men just get to wake up, get ready for work, and come home to a clean house and a hot meal. Women do everything else. Who's fucking idea was this? I've been doing it all for years, and I am exhausted.

I'm supposed to be a "boss bitch"—capable, engaged, and devoted to her family but also somehow simultaneously committed to self-growth. I should have a greater purpose than just raising my kids, but of course I should also be doing a great job at that. I am always measuring myself and even my kids against whatever peer group and falling short.

As a woman I feel the pressure to be quiet, attentive to my partner, skinny, pretty, supportive, and kind. I feel extremely judged and I keep what others see to the bare minimum.

I'm supposed to be an obedient and dutiful daughter, and sacrifice for my family. I'm supposed to behave and look good. As a mother, I feel the pressure to keep it all together and not drop the ball, despite this being the most difficult role of my life. I also feel the pressure to bring in income.

I snip, dye, conceal, slice, color, shrink, grow, contour, mutilate, pluck, shave, shave, shave, inject, fill, douse, spray, and starve myself. My value in this world is linked to my desirability. I have major people-pleasing tendencies. I'm supposed to be lithe, curvy, and beautiful. Even if we aren't beautiful, we should still be fuckable. I've been struggling against these expectations my entire life, trying to be something that I, as a fat woman, can never be.

I never feel attractive enough. I always want plastic surgery. I always feel dumb, despite having a PhD. I feel lazy because my chronic fatigue makes doing things very hard most of the time. As a woman, it feels like I'm supposed to be able to really hold it down, but when it comes to managing the house, I am very disorganized. I don't feel like a hard worker and I don't feel like I deserve career success. Most of the time, I feel like a failure.

Society wants women to be everything. It feels impossible.

Shame in the Home

Though we didn't go to church, my Catholic mother raised me under its influence. Obedient, modest, pretty but not beautiful, my mother was only as smart as girls were meant to be. She graduated from high school and waited to get married. In a time when feminists were fighting for a woman's right to work outside the home, my mother dreamt of no responsibility beyond raising her children and caring for her home.

Instead, she worked full-time as a secretary at a racetrack while my father cycled through jobs. We lived in the basement of her mother's home in Walton Hills, Ohio, a suburb on the east side of Cleveland. The squat, brown ranch wore all the calling cards of poverty. Broken-down cars were parked permanently in the driveway. The garage door hung halfway between open and shut. When the lawn mower broke, the lawn grew wild until the neighbors complained and the city threatened to issue a summons. The basement where my family lived flooded when it rained, turning the mocha-colored shag carpeting a dark soupy brown. In the corners of the rooms, wolf spiders built funneling nests. Black mold grew behind my mother's secondhand paperback copies of *Pride and Prejudice* and *Jane Eyre*.

Still, my mother had a deep and abiding faith in America, in its institutions and its ideals. A third-generation Polish immigrant, she believed that if people worked hard and lived right, anyone could share in the American Dream. This dream, for my mother as for most Americans of her generation, was epitomized by homeownership.

In the evenings in front of the TV, my mother pored over architectural magazines, planning construction of a house that would never be built. As a child on the couch alongside my mom, I pictured myself in the homes pictured in the magazines. I imagined we were different, better than I had already begun to fear we actually were.

While my mother struggled to manage the home, care for her children, and make ends meet, my father preserved a part of himself that did not belong to his family. He had drawers—literally one in every room—full of things belonging only to him. A drawer of toiletries in the bathroom. Vitamins in the kitchen. Food in the fridge only he was permitted to eat. As a little girl I would sneak into my father's bureau and fondle his silk ties. While the rest of us scrabbled over resources so limited it seemed as if everything in the house was broken, dirty, or used up, my father's belongings were ample and nice and totally off-limits.

I asked my female friends to recall the moment they realized they were a "girl." For many respondents, girlhood began with censure, injustice, and inferiority.

Debbie was eight years old, she tells me, when her mother told her she was no longer allowed to go shirtless: "I remember feeling confused, like I had done something wrong, but I didn't understand what."

Shannon was also around eight years old, she says, the first time she was told to hide her body. "I had a shirt that was too big for me and it hung down off my shoulder and showed my nipple. My mom said I couldn't wear it, and I was really confused, because when I was younger I would sometimes go without a shirt and it was no problem."

To be sure, bodies who are assigned male at birth are socialized to feel shame, but for different reasons that we will consider briefly later in this book, and little girls, more so than boys, are imbued from birth with an apprehension of wrongness, a fear of being "bad." Even when we're "good" and try our best to follow the rules, women and girls are denied opportunities and treated differently than our brothers.

"At the dinner table, there was always a noticeable difference in portion size between my brother and me," Eileen shares. "[My brother] had to deal with taking out the garbage and picking up the dog mess in the backyard, whereas my sisters and I shared cooking and housecleaning duties."

Her parents were both teachers and struggled to make ends meet. "So they told us early on they would only be able to pay for my brother's college tuition."

We're taught a girl's worth is measured primarily by her looks. Beauty is in opposition to intelligence, and girls aren't expected to be smart.

"When I was growing up, people were constantly insulting my intelligence," Renee says. "Dumb blonde, ditz, flaky. They made jokes. They were just jokes. No need to be offended. But I've spent much of my life internalizing that."

Even from homes where gender norms were more flexible, we get the message that girls are supposed to stay small, soft; remain unseen; not make a fuss; remain agreeable, polite and pleasing; and think of others before thinking of themselves.

As the oldest child and the only girl, Robin felt greatly rewarded for being smart, hardworking, and ambitious. She was encouraged to excel in and outside of school, expected to ace college and have a career.

At the same time, she says, "I was the only sibling expected to ever pick up a dirty shirt or stack a dishwasher, the only one told I'd have my knees broken if I ever smoked one cigarette, and the only one expected not to have sex too early."

The older we get, the more urgently it is impressed on us that living in a female body puts us at risk, and that it was our responsibility to ensure our own safety. Author Deb Caletti describes the feeling well in her novel *Girl, Unframed*. The narrator is catcalled and experiences "a heightened awareness of the bad shit that could happen if I wasn't careful."

Girlhood, as author Laurie Penny describes it in her book *Unspeakable Things*, is "a slow realisation that you are not considered as fully human as you hoped.

"You are a body first," Penny continues, "and your body is not yours alone: whether or not you are attracted to men, men and boys will believe they have a claim on your body, and the state gets to decide what you're allowed to do with it afterwards."

Shame in the World

In *The Shame Machine*, Cathy O'Neil argues "there's no greater power than shame to bring people into line." O'Neil contends that shame is sometimes healthy and justified, and she uses masking during the COVID-19 pandemic as an example. She shares an anecdote about a time during the height of the pandemic when a stranger berated her husband for walking down a public sidewalk without wearing a mask, arguing that someone who does not comply with a mask mandate can be shamed by their community into making the right choice.

The problem with this is that the right choice is rarely obvious. Even the example she uses of masks is complicated. At the beginning of the pandemic, people were discouraged from wearing them. The overall effectiveness of the mandate was debated, especially after restaurants reopened and we were allowed to take them off to eat and drink. Some people, like my special-needs son, couldn't tolerate them. After vaccinations became widely available and the pandemic dragged on for years, some people's risk tolerance went up and mask mandates were dropped, so the decision grew even more personal.

It's worth mentioning that, in O'Neil's example, her husband simply forgot. Did he really deserve castigation? Would someone shouting at you for making a mistake guarantee you wouldn't make that same mistake again?

We can't fall into line, as O'Neil suggests, because there is not one straight line; rather, we experience an endless number of lines intersecting one another. In fact, Brené Brown likens the ways social-community expectations function as being akin to a "web."

When we're children, understanding what is expected of us can be particularly confusing. Our parents contradicted themselves. The values we learned in the home collided with messages from the outside world. We don't always intuitively agree with the values being imposed on us—and we shouldn't.

If I took my mother's word for it, being a woman was just the best thing ever—and sure, sometimes girlhood has its perks. Adults took my innocence for granted. Disney promised me a prince. Before that happy ending, I'd be taken on a ton of fun dates, and they'd always pay. The fact that I was petite, my mother constantly reiterated, meant that I could fall in love with whatever boy I wanted and still wear heels.

But just underneath femininity's advantages lay an unspoken truth: almost anything associated with womanhood was at least a little embarrassing, from the soap operas women watched in the afternoon to the romance novels they read before bed. In the larger world, which filtered unmediated into our home, womanhood was insulted. Conversation between women was derided as gossip. Anything women enjoyed was forbidden: the food we ate was a "guilty pleasure." Women's clothing was restrictive and uncomfortable, or else you wore "mom jeans." Our place was in a kitchen, barefoot and pregnant. Even our cancer was pink.

As nice as it would feel to have a door opened for me every now and again, I realized that benevolent sexism—as I later came to call it—was a consolation, the goody bag you grabbed on the way out of a party you weren't invited to and had been asked to leave just as soon as you arrived.

It was a man's world. A boys' club. Girls were everything nice, but boys? Well, that was just men being men. I wouldn't have called it male privilege at the time, but I knew, even as a child: my father had something unavailable to my mother. What was available to my father, as a man, was far better than the world his wife and children inhabited. His was a world of possibility, a place far removed from moldy, beat-down, used-up reality—a place where people had *fun*.

After her parents divorced when she was age three, April lived with her father, a man she describes as a functioning meth addict.

"Doing methamphetamines encourages a spirit of disinhibition," April says. "There was all kinds of pornography left out. I saw many things that I wish I could erase from my memory, but they are just ingrained and burned so deeply."

Violence was commonplace, and April was a victim of neglect. She was a victim of sexual abuse at five years old, when she was touched inappropriately by an older child at the in-home daycare.

At eleven years old, she was introduced to the church: her pastor, Troy, and his wife, Jennifer, "were amazing parents to five beautiful children." They'd driven their family station wagon from their small, white town into Miller Park in Omaha, Nebraska, a poverty-stricken inner-city neighborhood, to tell the kids about Jesus.

Eventually, the evangelists purchased a van with a trailer and a speaker system to play gospel rap. They called it "Freedom Fun Club." Kids like April would play games and recite memorized scripture in exchange for prizes like candy and soda.

"They'd pick you up and take you to church on Sunday," April fondly recalls. "They brought hope. They accepted me and prayed for me—but they couldn't protect me."

April describes returning to her father's house afterward as a "personal nightmare." Entering the cold, dark space, she'd shuffle from the empty pantry to an empty fridge. There was no electricity or running water. "Sometimes, we'd run a hose from our neighbor Mrs. Shirley's house, fill the bathtub with water to flush the toilet if you went number two."

"I felt like an outcast, jealous and resentful towards God," April says. "I was taught that Jesus loved me so much and that nothing could ever separate me from his love. I was told my body was a sacred temple, yet I knew I had already been desecrated by men."

April did her best to keep her situation at home a secret, she says, but "it was not hard for those who started coming around to know that something was off." And yet, she says, "it was never off enough for anyone to ever call to get help or to have our situation be investigated."

Troy and Jennifer had moved on, and a different pastor was in charge on the day April went to her congregation with the news that she was pregnant. "I was shamed horribly," she says. "They made me feel so bad about myself."

As the pastor at the time lectured April, she took responsibility for what happened. "Even though I was supposed to be this child of God with this innocence and purity, I had become promiscuous at a very young age, trading my body for resources and attention."

April was removed from all her ministerial duties. "I was suicidal," she says. "I considered getting an abortion. I was ostracized from my church and from most of my friends."

April's story reflects how mixed messages can lead to shame, and the shame that comes when we feel a strong need to keep fundamental truths about ourselves and our experiences a secret. Even though Jenn didn't grow up in a religious community, she echoes having learned values similar to those held by my Christian friends, a belief that women are supposed to constantly self-sacrifice and abandon their own desires for the "greater good."

As Jenn puts it: "Self-sacrifice is idealized in Asian culture, which prioritizes collectivism and above all, the family.

"Women are supposed to be selfless and put others first, and if a woman chooses to spend time doing something that makes her happy and that takes time away from her kids, it's a huge problem."

Jenn's parents married in China, through kind of an arranged marriage, and came to the United States for a better life. She grew up in San Francisco's Chinatown, with her dad working as a busboy in a high-end Chinese restaurant her family could never afford to eat at.

After Jenn's dad got injured at the restaurant and could no longer work, Jenn's mother became a street artist, sketching portraits of tourists to provide for her family.

"I'm not sure who my dad was because he didn't express himself much," Jenn says, "but my mom was different. She was a lot of things you'd not think an Asian woman would be."

Jenn describes a childhood defined by dichotomies. She says she spent enormous amounts of time in front of the TV watching shows like *Saved by the Bell*, *Baywatch*, and *Beverly Hills 90210*, featuring older-looking girls obsessed with makeup. On *Baywatch*, women in swimsuits ran in slow motion down the beach.

Both the women on the TV and the obedient Asian woman archetype contrasted sharply with her mother, and the paintings she made in art class. "My mother was allowed to express herself, but I wasn't; there were all these paintings of nude bodies all over my house, but we can't talk about sex."

Then, Jenn says, "There was a chasm between this ideal of what a woman should look like versus me." She was scrawny, flat chested, with braces and really long, stringy hair. ("I looked like Cousin Itt.")

"It was cool to wear baggy jeans at the time," she says with a laugh. "Not a great look for someone that skinny. I was drowning in those clothes."

At fifteen years old, Jenn met her first boyfriend on the 30 Stockton bus.

When he asked for her number, she felt flattered—and ashamed: "I thought I looked ugly. I froze. It was a first."

They started hanging out at his house, and having sex.

"He didn't tell me that he came inside me, and of course I wasn't aware. When I found out I was pregnant, I couldn't tell my parents."

Teenage pregnancy was unacceptable, so she decided to have an abortion.

Sitting in the waiting room on the day of the procedure, Jenn clutched a Hello Kitty purse as if it were a life raft. "I remember being very numb. I had nowhere to process my feelings. I know now that you can numb yourself as a trauma response, but at the time I just thought, maybe I don't have any emotions.

"I never told my parents. My pediatrician had told them something, so I think they knew."

Jenn says she has still never discussed this experience with her parents. The shame of acknowledging this truth as a family, even decades later, would be too much.

Shame and Our Peers

Like so many women I spoke to, there was no age-appropriate talk of sex in my home. No meaningful sex ed at school either. The silence surrounding the subject, along with the mythical value of virginity, had the opposite of its intended effect.

After our initial encounter in the woods, Charlie started picking me up in the afternoons and bringing me back to his house. While his grandparents were away, most likely at work, Charlie and I made out on the couch. I'd strip naked, and we'd kiss. Sometimes I'd touch him through his clothes. When I did, he felt enormous to me, engorged and insistent, and I'd become terribly afraid—*dick shy*, the boys my age called it.

Charlie wasn't like a boy my age. He was sixteen, two years older, and so I trusted him to teach me what I was desperate to learn. I grew increasingly comfortable lying naked next to him, with him kissing me everywhere, expecting nothing in return. We barely talked, always getting right to business. He touched me, gently at first. Then harder. It was here that I learned my body's responses. It felt as if he knew just what to do. Slow or fast, he pushed his fingers inside of me, gently then harder.

One afternoon, as he was doing this, the living room began to spin. The ordinary day crumpled into itself, and, in one perfect moment, everything centered on the center of my body. Charlie whispered as it was happening, "You're having an orgasm."

Afterward, I was giddy. I didn't want to get dressed, maybe never. "You gotta!" Charlie said and threw me my shirt. "We gotta go," he insisted. "My grandpa's coming home!"

As bad luck would have it, the day of my first orgasm was the last time that Charlie and I "hung out." This was before anyone used the term "ghosting," and so I had no language to attach to the experience. He just stopped returning my pages. (Yes, I said "pages." C'mon, it was the 1990s.)

My encounter with Charlie set off a craving. From then on, I fell for one Shaggy look-alike after another, throwing my body at any boy that gave me even the slightest bit of attention. Ravenous for approval, I learned to put my partner's desires first. The only pleasure I came to expect would result from pleasing whatever boy I found myself with. I sought out sexual intimacy, even as every encounter left me feeling more and more devalued, dirtied, and detached from my body.

Somehow at school I maintained an image of innocence. I did not become a "slut," one of hundreds of words Melissa Febos rightly observed as being invented by men and used to maintain power over women and keep them in service to men. In *Girlhood*, Febos catalogs the challenges of navigating peer relationships, and the shame that comes with them. When she developed breasts and hips earlier than her peers, she was tortured—called names, spat on, prank-phone-called, and harassed. Febos cites a 2011 survey conducted by the American Association of University Women that found early development to be the most common attribute of sexually harassed students, followed closely by perceived prettiness.

Beauty can be a social liability, for sure, but those who do not fit into beauty stereotypes or follow beauty trends risk ostracization as well. In her memoir *Unbound*, Tarana Burke reflects on her encounters with the charge that she is ugly. "You can dodge a rock, but you can't un-hear a word," Burke writes. "You can't undo the intentional damage that some words have on your mind, body, and spirit."

As an adolescent, Reema lived in fear she'd be made fun of, called names and insulted, or become the subject of rumors or lies. Terrorized by stories from fifth-grade sleepovers where the popular girls would pour 7UP in one girl's hair or throw popcorn at her when she wasn't looking, she says she was grateful her parents made her leave early.

"They picked on one girl, Angela, mercilessly because she was so easy to get to," Reema recalls, "because she had a temper and because we knew her business. I don't know how we knew her father was in AA."

One time, Reema says, they put Angela's underwear in the freezer while she slept. "Forever for the rest of grammar school, Angela was that girl that got her underwear frozen."

At another sleepover, queen bee Brittany Banks had all the other girls in attendance to contribute to a note, unbeknownst to Reema. Brittany handed her the letter at the party.

"I was so naive," says Reema, recalling the pretty purple piece of paper with curly handwriting. "It was a list of 'Why Everybody Hates Reema.'"

A 2013 meta-analysis found that students who experience bullying are twice as likely as non-bullied peers to experience negative health effects such as headaches and stomachaches. A separate 2018 study found that peer stressors are a particularly strong predictor of depression. Multiple studies have found that bully-victims report more suicidal ideation and behaviors than uninvolved youth, including a 2008 Yale study which found that victims of bullying are between two to nine times more likely to consider suicide than non-victims.

Our so-called friends can be the death of us, literally. But peers can also be a much-needed salve. Teens buffer each other from the impacts of stressful relationships with parents. Girls, in particular, form close, albeit complex, bonds.

When April left her father's home at fourteen, she dropped out of school and started drinking and smoking pot. Her friends, she says, "pressured me into illegal activity, including drug dealing. There was gun violence. They pressured me into doing adult things," April says, including sexual activity that led to her unintended pregnancy. And yet, "Finding that place where I fit in was so amazing," she recalls. "I finally had people who would do anything for me, literally would kill for me, whereas my own family did nothing but put me in harm's way for their own gain."

Similarly, Jenn lights up when she describes the rave scene she discovered in high school. "I was with friends, it allowed me to feel a lot of unconditional love, and I think I needed that." After the abortion, her boyfriend dumped her—"I felt like a failure. I still wasn't able to have sad feelings for myself, but ecstasy gave me a lot of joy and I also smoked pot and it was awesome. It was a great escape from that shame."

Fatherless Daughters Unite

Haloed in blonde hair, with enormous blue eyes, Jeanetta was sexy. Though we were still children, grown men would lean their entire bodies out of car windows to whistle at her as we walked past. Kids our age noticed, too, of course, and I burned with envy watching

Jenny cycle disinterestedly through boyfriends. I didn't become popular myself, but because of my proximity to Jenny, I got a pass.

Jenny learned from her mother, Peggy, another version of what a woman could be. A single mom (a *divorcée* as my mom would say, the word dripping with subtext), Peggy wore Jenny's clothes, frosted the tips of her middle-aged hair, and worked nights as a waitress in what Jenny described as a "sleazy" bar. After school, Peggy would pick us up in her beat-up station wagon smoking Camel after Camel with all the windows rolled up until I'd just about die. I'd come home from a night at Jenny's and my mom would complain I smelled of smoke.

At some point, Jenny's mom married Paul, a guy Jenny hadn't even known Peggy was seeing. Jenny refused to attend the wedding. Before Paul there'd been Steve, and Jenny had liked Steve. Steve had been like a dad. Paul looked like a professional wrestler and drank cans of beer in the middle of the afternoon.

Instead of attending the wedding, Jenny and I spent that afternoon shoplifting, starting at JCPenney, where we went into the dressing room and put on layers and layers of clothes underneath our own. After that, we roamed through the drugstore, pocketing whatever we could—makeup, nail polish, candy, jewelry—things we didn't even want. It was like scratching at mosquito bites. Once we'd started, we scratched until we bled, until they scabbed and scarred. We didn't talk about it—its dirtiness, and the way that dirtiness made us feel grimy and good at the same time. On the walk home, we'd throw what we didn't want down the gutter.

The summer between our first and second years of high school, Jenny and I started talking about running away. We'd follow the railroad tracks that ran through the center of town, she said. We'd follow them to wherever they'd take us, living off Burger King Extra Value Meals and the free chips and salsa that Chi-Chi's gives you when you're waiting for your table. We had it all figured out. Compared to the other options I felt were available to me, taking off made sense. Jenny hated Paul and I was sick of shit at home—my parents fighting and what I would later come to understand as my brother's drug use. Jenny had a plan and, of all the people in my life, I could count on Jenny. She'd already started squirreling away travel-sized bottles of shampoo.

We didn't run away. Instead, before the heat of August broke, Jenny and I were back in the classroom, where fantasies of escape slipped away. School satisfied my need for structure. It was one place I felt I could control—a place where I believed I could succeed, if only I followed the rules. I had few friends besides Jenny, but teachers liked me and learning came easily. I was placed in gifted and talented classes, where I earned mostly A's. By junior year, Jenny and I had crawled our way up the ranks from junior varsity to varsity cheerleading.

That fall, Jenny and I started going dancing every Friday night at a club called the Cosmopolitan. The Cos, as we called it for short, was in a strip mall sandwiched between a Dollar Tree and a Payless shoe store. Week after week on under-twenty-one night, in a different tube top and the same skintight black pants, Jenny and I learned what it meant to be a woman. Attract attention. Smile. Be Nice.

Together, Jenny and I learned how to make men feel good about themselves, and how to handle the move-right-in-and-make-themselves-at-home types. We grew familiar with men who'd spend a whole conversation quoting some movie they'd seen that we hadn't. Men who'd make derogatory comments about all the other women in the bar. *Maybe*, we thought, *they weren't so bad. Maybe*, we thought, *we'd one day marry one of them.* We learned to smile and be nice as if our lives depended on it. *Maybe someday,* we intuitively understood, *they would.*

A month or so before high school graduation, I came home from school and my mother told me that my father was gone. For months he'd been traveling to and from Louisville, presumably for work. Now, just like that, my mom said he'd moved down there for good. I would later find out, I don't remember how, that he had another family. A new wife, a little girl. I cannot remember the last time I saw my father. No matter how hard I try.

Instead, I remember the evening I told my parents I had begun thinking of going to college. They were sitting together in the dark on the couch in the living room in front of the TV when I nervously approached them. I remember the sound of the canned laughter. I see my father's face illuminated by the flashing screen. I'd been awarded a two-hundred-dollar scholarship by the local chapter of the Veterans for Foreign Wars for second place in an essay contest. The theme: what freedom means to me. I can't remember what I wrote, only that it was important I win.

Years later, when I first started writing professionally, I avoided the subject of my father. I did not want to think, let alone admit, I was just another stripper with "daddy issues," a character I derided as a victim and a cliché. As a child, I didn't know that people came from different homes. I thought that there was "normal" and "not normal," and that my family was "not normal." I didn't want anyone to know.

For a long time, I reacted very strongly against the assertion that all women with experiences in the sex trades are victims of childhood sexual abuse, a characterization frequently perpetuated by anti-sex-worker feminists who think they are advocating for women and girls by speaking on our behalf. It reinforces painful stereotypes about sex workers. It's insulting and it's just plain wrong: I was never molested as a kid.

Shame kept me from admitting my more complicated truth. Throughout my girlhood, my mother over-relied on me for intimacy and emotional support, and so I knew too much about her and my father's sex life, including details of my father's extramarital affairs. These details from my childhood are examples of what psychologists would call "covert sexual abuse," as are even more commonplace experiences, such as a parent idolizing their daughter's beauty or commenting on her body in relation to men.

British academic and writer Katherine Angel's book *Daddy Issues* is a takedown of the term, which is frequently invoked to mock a woman's choice of sexual partner, whether due to his age, looks, status, or power, ultimately suggesting she's fallen for some version of her dad. Angel examines the portrayal of fathers in stories and film, as well as contemporary fathers in our peripheral vision, men like Harvey Weinstein and Donald Trump—villainous characters we can't imagine calling "dad."

In her analysis, Angel looks at why women are so often driven to defend abusive fathers who have damaged them but to whom they cannot help but feel attached. We identify and idolize our fathers, even as we may be intellectually repulsed by them. No matter how not-good-enough your parents are, Angel suggests, we never stop loving them and seeking their approval.

I was fortysomething years old when Angel's book gave me permission to feel the way I felt toward my father. It was not my fault. Angel shone a light on how women are made to bear personal responsibility for the harm inflicted on us by men, starting too often with our shitty dads, and suggested that even girls with intact relationships with their fathers have been impacted by a culture that glorifies men no matter their behavior.

Today, the phrase "daddy issues" holds no power over me, but for years, the mere thought of my father triggered feelings of worthlessness and, yes, shame. I was confused, angry, and afraid of what my father's actions said about me.

The spring semester of my junior year of high school, I met the man that would become my fiancé, an affable guy named Rick. Rick went to a Catholic school and came from what I considered a good family—the kind of family that ate dinner at the dinner table and not in the living room in front of the TV. The kind of people that said grace. The first time Rick and I went out, he brought me carnations from the supermarket where he worked as a bag boy, and we actually *went out*—not just to the woods to make out but to Burger King, where he paid for my meal.

After our first date, he kissed me politely on my doorstep. The crickets, the dim yellow porch light, moths throwing themselves against the bulb—it all gave me the strange sensation of being filmed. Not like in a porn—which is how I typically felt around a guy—but as if I were an actress and we were both following the script of a very pleasant movie. Rick was, I thought, what I'd always been looking for: a guy that could look my mother in the eye.

The same semester that Rick and I started dating, a guidance counselor suggested I consider Antioch College. The fall semester of my senior year, my mom took me for a campus visit. Together, my mother and I walked across a campus where students lay on blankets under shady trees, reading books. Tulips bloomed around the main building. It was all so picturesque, so civilized. During my admissions interview, I learned about the school's cooperative education model and the concept of experiential learning. At Antioch, I would be taught to trust life experience as a valuable source of knowledge and insight. Students weren't given grades, the admissions counselor explained. Instead, professors wrote narrative evaluations and students wrote self-evaluations, and both appeared on the transcripts, bearing equal weight.

It was very different from the public school I came from, Bedford High, which required students to enter through metal detectors and wear picture IDs, and which was notorious for a pack of students beating to death the bus driver of a visiting rival basketball team.

This was where I wanted to go, no matter the cost: thirty thousand dollars per year, exactly my mother's annual salary. To her credit, my mother sprang to life and made it her mission to see that I entered every high school essay contest and applied for every scholarship that I could. With my mother's help, I paid for my entire first year with scholarships and other merit-based aid. In a world surrounded by shame (even if I didn't yet have the language to describe it as such), this was something that I could be very proud of. And I was.

The Girls Are Not Alright—But They Will Be

Telling our stories is reparative. Even as it makes me vulnerable to judgment, I talk about shame. I tell and retell my story. Each time, I see myself in a new, if not shameless, then shame-less light. This is the beginning of our recovery: learning to feel every feeling and seizing our power without fear. It starts by finding places and people that won't reject or abandon you, and with whom you can share your true self.

Sometimes that starts alone, in a journal. "Writing is where I leave my state of suspended animation, and start on my own life," writes Katherine Angel at the conclusion of *Daddy Issues*. "It is where I refuse the expectation of compliance, and where I can feel my aggression. It's where I go to be deeply and freely alone; to create myself, and experience myself as real."

Sometimes that's finding a just-right friend. As Reema said, "I always had one friend. That one good friend I could be myself with, and so I was okay."

Sometimes it starts by leaving home and finding a larger, wider community—at college, in a new city, or with a new group or identity. For me, my time at Antioch, and my exposure to more and different people, helped me start to find and then share my true self, without shame.

Without that safe space, kids are not okay. Girls today, in particular, are in crisis. A 2023 study of teenage girls' mental health conducted by the Centers for Disease Control and Prevention found that girls are presenting unprecedented levels of depression and suicidality. To be sure, the pandemic was a factor, but the results of the 2023 survey echoed previous surveys and reports that began prior to the coronavirus crisis. A 2020 study by the CDC, for example, reported that, between 2007 and 2018, the national suicide rate among youth aged 10 to 24 increased 54 percent. A separate 2020 CDC report found that high-school-aged girls, and Black girls in particular, as well as LGBTQ youth, had the highest increase in suicide attempts compared to other demographics. Of the more than 17,000 US high school students surveyed in the fall of 2021, more than half of the girls reported persistent hopelessness—double that of the boys. Most concerning, the surveys revealed that one in three seriously considered suicide, and one in ten attempted it. We know from rafts of research that girls with comorbidity are at the greatest risk. Girls with ADHD, for example, are three to four times more likely to attempt suicide than girls without this diagnosis. This is according to a 2021 study published in the journal *Archives of Suicide Research*.

In the groundbreaking book *The Body Keeps the Score*, psychiatrist and trauma specialist Bessel van der Kolk explains precisely why girls who witness domestic violence grow up at a higher risk of ending up in violent relationships themselves (boys risk becoming abusers), and why girls who experience neglect and abuse are significantly more likely to be raped in later life. The reason for the increased likelihood is not some inherent defect in females, as some may believe, but rather because trauma begets trauma. Earlier traumatic experiences literally shape the brain in ways that make an individual more vulnerable to future harm.

An impulse takes root and becomes a neural pathway. Unspoken shame turns into unbearable feelings of loneliness, despair, and rage. Rage with nowhere to go gets directed at the self as depression, self-hatred, and self-destructive acts.

Without intervention, girls who experience high levels of shame can suffer negative effects for the rest of their lives: cognitive defects, depression, disassociative symptoms, troubled sexual development, self-mutilation, abnormal stress-hormone responses, physical illness, psychiatric diagnosis, and the list goes on.

What do we do to help our daughters? And yes, I'm talking to all women, because whether or not you're a mother, you have a hand in raising the next generation of girls.

Well, for starters, we need to increase sexual education. Only twenty-nine states in the US mandate sexual education. And, in fact, thirty-seven states require abstinence to be taught as the only way to prevent pregnancy and sexually transmitted diseases. Folks argue that it ought to be taught in the home, but as journalist Kat Tenbarge quipped on Twitter, "Can parents name every STD and how they're transmitted? Can they teach you how to identify date rape drugs? Can they define 'pelvic floor'? And more importantly—would they?"

We need to confront our shame and honestly interrogate our sexual experiences, including the stuff that happened to us when we were young. We have to educate ourselves, because we can't teach our children information and skills that we ourselves lack. For those of us raised in homes that viewed sex with disgust, we need to get over our hang-ups. This doesn't mean uncritical acceptance. Sex-positive culture pushed back against the notion that sex is inherently dirty and dangerous, but as Rebecca Traister put it in a 2015 article for *The Cut* titled "Why Sex That's Consensual Can Still Be Bad. And Why We're Not Talking About It," the "exuberant, raunchy, confident, righteously unapologetic, slut-walking ideology that sees sex—as long as it's consensual—as an expression of feminist liberation" results in "a neatly halved sexual universe, in which there is either assault or there is sex positivity." This left us no way to account for a lifetime of distressing or simply lackluster sex and complicated sexual experiences.

Part of sexual education is thinking more critically about gender. Our conception of what it means to be a boy or girl (or something in-between) is evolving, but slowly. We need to think critically of the messages we're sending, and honestly examine the toll it takes. Barbies may come in more varied body sizes and skin tones, but as British feminist and author Laura Bates examined in the *Guardian*, the products that the STEM Kit Barbie builds are limited almost entirely to the realm of fashion and household chores: dresses, a moving clothes rack, a shoe rack, a jewelry holder, and a washing machine.

"And, yes, they're all pink," observes Bates.

What's wrong with the color pink? you might ask. Well, nothing, necessarily. My daughter loves all things feminine. I don't deny her the L.O.L. Surprise dolls she's obsessed with. At the same time, I recognize that her interest in makeup (at three years old!) is not innate.

Even seemingly innocent traditions send an unintended message. As Caroline Kitchener reported for the *Lily*, the time-honored American tradition of father-daughter dances is rooted in an expectation that fathers have so little in common with their daughters that these types of activities need to be invented, noting that there are no such rituals marking the time that fathers spend with their sons.

So long as the girls' section of clothing stores remains a sea of pastels, spaghetti straps, short skirts, padded bras, and thongs for very young girls, we shouldn't be surprised when our daughters internalize certain expectations. We must push back when schools impose restrictive dress codes that put the onus on little girls for "distracting" their male peers.

Most of all, we need to take shame out of the parenting toolbox. As a mother, I get it; we want to protect our children. But in the words of parent coach Kristin Gallant and licensed marriage and family therapist Deena Margolin, cocreators of Big Little Feelings: "Fear is a terrible teacher." Shame may work in the moment—your kid will freeze and stop the behavior right then, a recent Instagram post reads, but only because a trauma response kicks in. Shame won't help our children do better next time—just as it didn't help us when we were kids. Instead, it will erode their self-worth and resilience, and it will make them more likely to hurt and shame themselves and others.

How many of us grew up hearing things like "I don't like your attitude," "You are so ungrateful," or even "I am so disappointed in you"? As parents, we may have said similar things ourselves.

Instead of shaming our children, we need to give them permission to tell their truth. I want to be the mom my daughter comes to when she's got a problem. When she's struggling with something, I want her to think, *Mom will know just how to help me* and not *Mom would never understand.*

No, as a parent, I'm not perfect. Of course I'm not. I don't have to be—and neither do you. When I make a mistake as a mom, I model self-forgiveness. I teach my daughter by example that it's never too late to accept all parts of ourselves, including our shame.

3

Entertainment Tonight

How the Humiliation of "Bad" Women Affects Us All

Sometime during the first semester of my first year in college, my childhood best friend Jenny called me long distance to let me know she'd started a new job. She'd begun working at the Crazy Horse, a strip joint in a row of strip joints in a part of town known only for its strip joints. The color left my face.

That semester, I'd enrolled in my first women's studies course. Everything I was being taught about sex work contradicted what I knew about Jenny. I pictured my beautiful best friend since forever, exploited, working in the kind of place that decent women—girls like her and me, I thought—would picket to shut down.

When I said as much to Jenny, she very politely told me to fuck off.

"What the hell do you know?" she said.

There I sat, in the common room of my dorm, while Jenny was somewhere back in Bedford, Ohio—at her mom's house still, I think, or at her apartment, if this was during a time that she was living with her boyfriend. She was right: I'd never so much as been in a strip club.

Still, I hung up and cried. Of everything I had been led to believe that a sex worker could be, Jenny was none of it. She was smart and funny, beautiful inside and out—the toughest bitch I'd ever met.

She was my best friend, and I didn't want to lose her.

And so, that winter break, my boyfriend Rick and I visited Jenny at work. The place looked like a normal bar. It was not at all how I thought a strip club would look. No one looked sad. The men weren't rude. Everyone looked like they were having a great time, and why not? It was like all the clubs Jenny and I had spent our whole girlhood waiting to be let into. At nineteen years old, we still weren't old enough to enter most bars. Not only were girls our age allowed into strip clubs, but they were getting paid to be there.

When Jenny came over, she explained how it worked. She answered all my questions: Can the guys touch? No. Do you have to take off your bottoms? Yes. What do you do if you have your period? You stick in a tampon, and you cut off the string. What if a guy's being an asshole? You walk away.

In the car on the way home, Rick and I made fun of Jenny. I told my mom the place was gross. I told Jenny and everyone else my opinion hadn't changed, but by the end of that night, a seed had been planted. All my life, I had wanted nothing more than my mother's approval. I still wanted that. I wanted, so badly, to be good. But I saw the attention Jenny was getting and the money she made . . . and I wanted that, too.

. . . .

The biblical story of Jezebel is a cautionary tale. The daughter of the priest-king Ethbaal, she, along with her husband, King Ahab, ruled the kingdom of Israel and is said to have promoted the worship of false gods, harassed and killed God's prophets, and arranged for an innocent man to be falsely charged and executed. The Lord let King Ahab off the hook, and Jezebel took the blame for both their crimes.

On reckoning day, the Bible tells us "she put on eye makeup [and] arranged her hair" before the eunuchs threw her out a window and she plummeted to her death.

Even though biblical scholars concede there is no scriptural evidence that she was a prostitute or even an unfaithful wife, Jezebel was branded a whore. She was marked as an enemy of God for using her womanly ways to gain a place in the government, and she was found guilty of pride, selfishness, and greed.

Similarly, the modern-day jezebel is considered sexually promiscuous, controlling, impudent, and morally unrestrained. A jezebel's presence doesn't just suggest sex—she is an instigator of sex, a character who revels in her promiscuity. A jezebel is shameless, it is said, and to be so is a crime that makes one as dangerous as Judas.

On the subject of contemporary jezebels, there are too many to list, but let's just start with one of the most recent and vivid examples. She is an accomplished actress, a vocal and politically astute humanitarian, and yet, sadly, Amber Heard is and will probably remain best known as Johnny Depp's ex-wife.

In May 2016, Heard filed for divorce after fifteen months of marriage, citing irreconcilable differences and alleging that she was the victim of emotional, verbal, and physical abuse. From the outset, Heard's mistreatment was illustrative of how survivors are typically victimized. She was disbelieved and blamed, her grief put on display. And the more she begged for privacy, the more she was accused of bringing it all on herself.

In spite of—or, you might say, because of—the abuse, Heard

became an outspoken advocate for victims and survivors of interpersonal violence. In November 2016, Heard filmed an emotional public service announcement for the #GirlGaze Project referring generally to her own experience as a survivor. That December, she published an essay in *Porter* magazine once again encouraging survivors to speak out, even as she acknowledged the backlash they would likely endure.

Then, in 2018, Heard collaborated with the ACLU to produce an op-ed for the *Washington Post*. In the 762-word piece, Heard spoke broadly of her experiences as a survivor in order to highlight the issue of how institutions protect men accused of sexual violence and domestic abuse. In response and seemingly without any sense of the irony, Depp sued Heard for defamation, accusing Heard "and her friends in the media" of orchestrating a "sexual violence hoax."

Depp's legal strategy was an abuse tactic that therapists refer to as DARVO: Deny, Attack, Reverse it all as if they are the Victim and you are the Offender. Heard was branded an opportunist and a gold digger, untrustworthy and unstable. Various mental health diagnoses were weaponized against her, including borderline and histrionic personality disorders. The onslaught had its intended effect: Heard said she felt "humiliated," and described the online criticism of her testimony as "agonizing."

Agonizing is how it felt, watching it happen. Although I purposely didn't follow the trial, it was impossible to avoid. Reels appeared in my Instagram feed, and before I knew it, I was watching a woman's reputation being systematically torn apart in a public forum. It was upsetting, and it was all too familiar.

There's a saying I've heard: it's not personal, even when it's got your name on it. I could imagine some of the shame and humiliation. I thought back to my own experiences, when I was christened the "prosti-teacher" and media outlets were inexplicably sharing slide-shows of my personal Facebook photos on their news sites. When you're in the thick of it, shame can feel so personal. But Amber Heard wasn't the first "bad" woman to be publicly humiliated—and, sadly, she already hasn't been the last. Throughout history, countless women have been burned at the stake. Every day, another woman is politi-cally sacrificed in the news and on social media for stepping out of line. All these characters of women, all the way back to the Bible, serve a malevolent purpose in our cultural imagination. Public ag-gression toward and public shaming of a woman, even an imperfect one—nay, especially, an imperfect one—has an impact on us all.

Women Are on Trial (Even When They're Not)

The first time I remember seeing a woman humiliated in the media I was twelve years old, as the Anita Hill hearings played on TV. Like much of the viewing audience, adolescent or otherwise, I was titil-lated by the details the law professor was compelled to recount—Long Dong Silver? Pubic hair in a Coke?!—and yet, even to a child, the idea that a man in power might so recklessly abuse his privilege was not at all surprising.

My own mother, then a secretary at a racetrack, described the many offices where she'd worked as "boys' clubs." The subjugation of women in the workplace was, I understood, just the way things were.

Anita's testimony before the committee was met with indifference, disinterest, condescension, and outright hostility. She was character-ized as a scorned woman, a Civil Rights zealot, and, yes, a jezebel.

But Anita was none of these things. Watching her speak for

herself on the television, even to a child, that was clear. Hill spoke in faith that her individual story was relevant and that it brought to light a deeper, systemic issue. The harassment she had endured was not just her problem but *our* problem. She spoke calmly and confidently, knowing the solution was to speak out. Despite, and in some ways *because* of, all she went through, I believed Anita Hill.

I wish I could say I had the same sense of clarity when the news networks made a mockery of Monica Lewinsky. Instead, I found myself silently agreeing with the mobs who made fun of the twenty-four-year-old intern's appearance. I have vague memories of mothers, including probably my own, joining their husbands in blaming a young woman for her transgression, rather than the adult man involved, as if the greatest moral failing happening here was a child falling short of society's aesthetic ideals.

We think of shame as the consequence of our own bad choices, reserved for people who've made questionable decisions (people like me, I'm sure at least some readers are thinking—someone dumb enough to have bragged in print about a sex-work past). We want to believe, to paraphrase Cathy O'Neil, that as a society we direct shame toward people behaving badly, and that if people make dumb choices and carry on with their defects, shame is a matter of course.

By the time we all met Monica in that cringeworthy beret, I had fully absorbed these lessons society teaches us about shame. I had also absorbed certain notions about womanhood easily summed up in our collective criticisms of Monica: don't be slutty, stupid, or fat.

Anita Hill has been described as the perfect victim. She was highly educated, erudite, and attractively dressed. While an argument can be made that, for some, her Blackness undermined her appearance of innocence, for the rest of us, the facts were cut and dry. Hill unequivocally rejected her superior's advancements. She passed a polygraph test. Try as they might to paint her as a provocateur, she was a victim.

She was a *victim*, and still they chewed her up.

We Have a History of Humiliating Women

Hill and Lewinsky were two of the first, but they were hardly the last. Growing up in the '90s and '00s, there was a steady parade of women upon whom society could cast judgment.

In 1992, one year after Anita Hill, a seventeen-year-old girl named Amy Fisher became the "Long Island Lolita" after she shot and severely wounded the wife of the much older auto-body-shop owner, Joey Buttafuoco, with whom she'd been having an affair. In a 2003 interview with CBS News, Fisher described Buttafuoco as a predator and disclosed she was already vulnerable when she met him, as she had previously been sexually abused, and that she was struggling with low self-esteem when the thirty-six-year-old mechanic "was able to maneuver his way into my life." In spite of her age and the circumstances, Fisher was charged with first-degree murder and portrayed as a cold and calculated vixen. Her story was made into not one but three TV movies, two of which aired on the same night.

One year later, a "hot-blooded Latina," Lorena Bobbitt, became tabloid fodder after she cut off her husband's penis, an event so presumably hilarious it overshadowed the fact that she'd been a victim of years of physical and sexual abuse.

Like Bobbitt, singles figure skater and Olympic hopeful Tonya Harding was characterized as a quick-tempered hussy after her teammate Nancy Kerrigan was attacked after practice by an uniden-tified man. Framed as a catfight of epic proportions between Hard-ing, a jealous and impulsive "white-trash waitress" and "America's ice princess" Kerrigan, the brutal assault on Kerrigan was character-ized as the culmination of a long and fractious public rivalry be-tween the two skaters. It was, in fact, Harding's ex-husband who coordinated the attack on Kerrigan, but the way many remember it, Harding swung the solid-metal baton.

Did the facts even matter? These women weren't people, they were *characters*. It was *fun*. Sure, men were involved—but the women were spotlighted—and women are never taken seriously, no matter how serious their crimes.

On the subject of serious crimes, there's "Foxy Knoxy" Amanda Knox, the twenty-year-old American student found guilty of the murder of her roommate, Meredith Kercher, in Umbria, Italy, in 2007. We are less likely to know that Knox was ultimately exoner-ated than we are to remember the TV movies re-creating how she *might've* committed the crime. Italian prosecutors painted her mo-tive as a threesome gone wrong. As proof of guilt, they pointed to a closed-circuit TV that caught Knox doing a cartwheel in the hall-way at the police station while waiting to be questioned—which is definitely the sort of weird shit I'd have done at her age.

These women were young and many had trauma histories prior to their infamy. None of them asked to be celebrities. Instead, they were normal women thrust into the news because something terrible happened. Some of them had a part in bringing about those terrible circumstance, and others didn't. Either way, the media coverage was cruel, deliberately irresponsible, and undeniably wrong.

Women Behaving "Badly"

It would also be easy to blame the media makers—because, to a certain extent, it's true: media empires make enormous profits off these shaming stories. As a journalist, I know the difficulty in getting a counternarrative past gatekeepers, who were (and still are) overwhelmingly men.

But I suspect it's more than this.

In the introduction to her seminal text *Making News*, American sociologist Gaye Tuchman describes how most media portray women, if at all, in traditional roles: we are homemakers and mothers, or, if we are in the paid workforce, clerical and other "pink-collar" jobs. There are few, if any, depictions of strong female characters in positions of responsibility or authority, Tuchman noted, even inside the home. Tuchman's work was published in 1978, but to an extent it remains true to this day. Women's magazines often still focus on "domestic" pursuits such as marriage and child-rearing. Even in emerging media, there is a huge appetite for women in traditional roles. ("With her flawless locks and perfectly appointed nursery in various shades of ecru, with nary an errant Lego or Cheerio in sight," EJ Dickson writes in *Rolling Stone*, "[the "Momfluencer"] has been a figure of both derision and immense authority, with all other mothers parenting in her indomitable shadow.") Almost half a century later, there remains a dearth of media aimed at women that encourages education, training, and other choices that tend to bring individuals into positions of power, authority, and independence. Movies, magazines, TV shows—hell, the real-life conversations I have with friends—still don't pass the Bechdel test.

But stories of women behaving badly pierce through.

It makes sense, given the glut of honest conversations. With all the suppression and self-censure, there is a ravenous public appetite for stories about women who defy the rules. And it is no wonder the audience, and women in particular, feel pulled in by these narratives. All those urges we so deeply resisted. All the times we didn't. *She did.*

When you hear a story about a woman who broke the rules, who raised her voice, who screwed the boss (metaphorically or literally), who castrated (again, metaphorically or literally) her abuser, it's no wonder we feel drawn in, disgusted, curious, and confused. Maybe even a little jealous. We as a society are deeply ambivalent about women with seemingly enough power to be bad.

There's a Human Being Behind the Headline

"Everybody was very quick to be like, Oh, she wanted this. She's a fame whore. She wanted to be famous, and she orchestrated this whole thing." Sydney laughs. "The reality was that I never wanted that kind of attention. If you ask any of my friends or family, I'm very introverted. I'm a homebody. I'm, like, the last person that would want to call all that attention on herself."

I would have never uttered those words myself in the aftermath of my "unmasking." To my shame, I have always been—as the *New York Post* once called me in one photo caption—an "attention whore." But this young woman who found herself in similar circumstances a few years later was most certainly not.

News coverage at the time will tell a different story. In interviews at the time, Sydney Leathers says she met then-NYC mayoral candidate Anthony Weiner on social media—and that *she* initially reached out to *him*, because she was a fan. How else could she explain how they first met, without revealing the stigmatizing truth that she was a sex worker?

More than a decade later, Sydney tells me a different story. Sydney was twenty-two years old and working at a law firm, when she logged on to Seeking Arrangements, an online dating service that connects attractive younger women and older men willing to pay for their company—"you know, to make extra money just to make ends meet," Sydney said.

"It was purely like a survival thing in my mind that I thought was very temporary," she explained. "I wasn't savvy; I had no friends that were sex workers. It was like this big secret."

Sydney talks a little about "Anthony," as he introduced himself, and what he promised. "He starts carrot dangling. I am too stupid and naive at this point to know, get money up front, even if they're a rich person, you know. I was just young and stupid."

They never met in person, and he never bought Sydney any gifts or paid her so much as a penny. Still, they continued messaging for months, until—as Sydney puts it—she felt "kind of weirdly trapped in this situation, not knowing how to end it."

From the very start, Anthony brazenly shared intimate details of his life with Sydney. He contacted her from his work email account, she says, and made no effort to hide that he was a very public figure. Anthony was Anthony Weiner, former representative for New York's 9th congressional district. He was beginning another run for mayor of New York City, in spite of a sexting scandal in 2011 and after two previous mayoral runs, in 2005 and 2009. He must've been proud of himself, because the day Weiner was featured in *People* magazine, Sydney says he sent her a copy.

The celebrity weekly interviewed Weiner alongside his wife, Huma Abedin, and addressed the earlier lewd text and photo scandal that had led to his resignation from Congress. Oblivious that her husband was still up to no good, Abedin spoke earnestly of what it took for them "to get to where [they] are today," presenting Weiner as a devoted husband and doting father to a six-month-old.

Maybe he expected Sydney to be impressed. Instead, she was repulsed: "I remember, this was like the turning point for me. He's on the cover of *People* magazine with his wife talking about how he's a changed man. And he doesn't do any of the sexual behaviors from before." Meanwhile, they'd been sexting for a month. She paused. "I don't like hypocrites."

That's when Sydney says she sent a bunch of the information about her correspondence with Anthony to a gossip blog, *The Dirty*.

Now at this point you may be asking, "What was she thinking?" It's a question I've personally been confronted with time and again. Remember we're talking about a twenty-two-year-old. She was offended by this "creepy, lying public figure" and thought she could use the media to redress his behavior without the institution turning on her, a relative no one.

"I asked to remain anonymous, which [*The Dirty*] honored." Some days after they broke the story, Sydney says, "A stranger messaged me on Facebook, and sent me the link to the *BuzzFeed* story and was like, Oh, you're gonna be famous. And I was like, What?"

BuzzFeed had outed her, including her full legal name and photos from her Facebook, everything.

"The next month was horrible," Sydney says. "It was insane. Every tabloid was in my city, literally stalking me. They camped out outside my apartment." Sydney had no savings, no family to fall back on, few friends. She had just started therapy to address childhood trauma. Now, paparazzi reported breathlessly on her every move. "They went to the spray-tanning salon where I went. They interviewed people at my hometown taco dive, they contacted everyone I followed on social media. It was such an invasion of privacy," Sydney says, "on a level I could not comprehend."

Listening to Sydney, my whole body understands the overwhelming terror she must have been feeling. It takes me back to my own brush with tabloid "fame," and my belief—incredibly misguided, it turns out—that truth and justice would prevail. As Sydney puts it, "I was so naive."

I could relate to Sydney's shame and self-recrimination. For days after my own experience in the glare of the tabloid headlines—in the immediate aftermath of the initial "Hooker Teacher" headlines—paparazzi parked outside my apartment, and telescopic lenses pointed straight into my semi-parted curtains. I felt violated, and afraid. Caricaturized in the media, I felt outraged, indignant. I was incensed. Then-mayor Michael Bloomberg suggested the city was pursuing legal actions against me, as if I'd done something illegal for speaking publicly about my years-prior actions, and he said that he personally called for my reassignment to administrative duties ("We're just not going to have *this woman* in front of a class," he said).

Dr. Christine Marie is an expert on misrepresentation in the media, which she describes as a unique traumatic experience with a profoundly negative impact on multiple aspects of one's life. In 2020, she wrote her doctoral thesis on the subject, and she has been working as a trauma-sensitive media and psychology consultant, educator, and life coach ever since.

She is also a victim—initially of cult-based human trafficking and then of blowback from the media and the public when she dared to speak up and share her story. In 2013, Marie agreed to participate in an interview for what she believed was a reputable television network.

"It took me a decade to find the courage to agree to do this," Marie writes in her thesis. "[Publicity] was not something I sought out. After years of therapy, study, and conversations . . . I came to believe that by publicly sharing my experience, I was exhibiting personal strength."

Instead of feeling redeemed by her appearance, "when the episode aired before millions of potential viewers worldwide, my story was drastically twisted. I was turned into a character in a fictional story with circumstances I did not even recognize, yet it was touted as a true story."

Marie says the production blamed her for her own victimization, and she was ridiculed on social media. "Comments about the episode were filled with shaming refrains of how I was the cause of all the harms against me, and I deserved it all," Marie says. "I was mortified."

Beyond the very material costs associated with the loss of one's reputation, there's an incalculable emotional toll. Humiliation, even more than shame, is strongly associated with depression. Victims of media humiliation, including cyberbullying and online harassment (including trolling, stalking, revenge porn, doxing, and other forms of online aggression and cruelty), suffer from feelings of anguish and despair.

Repairing one's reputation, Marie wrote, can feel as impossible as "trying to gather up the feathers of a down feather pillow ripped open during a tornado.

"Since I could not erase the degrading content from the internet, I saw no way to escape the humiliating misinformation permanently branded on my character by the search engines. My credibility was gone." Her thoughts turned to suicide.

Media misrepresentations more frequently and more negatively impact trauma survivors and marginalized populations, including women and other historically objectified and dehumanized groups. Misrepresentation can be a secondary victimization. Stories about domestic violence survivors, victims of rape and sexual assault, or survivors of commercial sexual exploitation deserve sensitivity, accuracy, and respect. Speaking from experience, misrepresentation feels like a second betrayal and magnifies the self-blame.

Calling Out "Call Out Culture"

Twenty years after Brené Brown declared a war on shame, our culture of shame continues to rage out of control. We see instances of shaming on social media, in op-ed columns, and in our local communities, and we personally experience shame more frequently and more acutely than ever. From celebrities and reality TV stars to everyday civilians, women remain the subject of daily "controversies." Legitimate arguments devolve into sexist attacks.

A 2020 mixed methods study published in *Sex Roles* found 2.9 million tweets in one week contained one of four sexist slurs ("bitch," "slut," "cunt," and "whore"). That's 419,000 sexist slurs a day. Many of these hostile messages were written, retweeted, and liked by networks of cyberbullies who tend to attack celebrities, but sexist slurs appeared in smaller, everyday conversations as well. According to researchers, sexist tweets denigrate nonnormative behavior and maintain patriarchal culture and attitudes, and contribute to an antagonistic environment that targets women and femmes.

In other words, every hostile message that is tweeted, retweeted, and liked—whether aimed at a celebrity or civilian—sends a message and contributes to our culture of shame. We tell ourselves we're "punching up," but privileged or not, even a woman as powerful as Gwyneth Paltrow wrestles with feelings of inadequacy. (She said it herself, in a 2021 interview with the *New Yorker*: "I drive myself really hard to not age and to not be disappointed in the way I look, and I'm still disappointed in the way I look.")

Madonna may be resilient enough to withstand criticism, but the rest of us in aging bodies are watching the feeding frenzy of media coverage of the 2023 Golden Globes describing her "fucked up" and "freaky" face. Every time we take a sexist survey of a woman's appearance or conduct—celebrity or not—it reinforces a gendered message about who, how, and what we're allowed to be.

It's no wonder, to our shame, that we are obsessed with our looks. According to a 2021 study conducted by Rosalind Gill of City, University of London, 90 percent of women and nonbinary folks are digitally altering their images. We're evening out our skin tone, reshaping our features, whitening our teeth, and shaving off weight to experience a sense of belonging by conforming to what society calls beautiful.

We filter what we say, too.

"I am really careful with what I post or who I friend online," said one woman I interviewed.

"It takes me forever to post something on social media," another friend admits. Fearful of making a mistake or saying the wrong thing, she says, "I will rewrite and rewrite a post a million times or I will keep it incredibly short. I usually just end up deleting whatever it is I was trying to say and saying nothing."

It's not that these and other folks I spoke to were afraid of criticism. They are afraid of an audience that is inherently hostile, a culture of shame that seizes on another person's vulnerabilities as a way of making themselves look and feel better about themselves.

Video essayist and cultural critic Natalie Wynn defines "cancel culture" as the "online shaming, vilifying, and ostracizing of prominent members of a community by other members of that community."

At the start of a nearly two-hour YouTube video on the term's history and current usage, Wynn says that "canceling" someone "started out as this vigilante strategy for bringing justice and accountability to powerful people who previously had been immune to any consequences for their actions," and offers the #MeToo movement as an example of the good that social media shaming can do.

"The promise of canceling was that it was going to give power back to people who had none, and bring justice to prominent abusers," Wynn says. "It's, in a way, the twenty-first-century version of the guillotine—the bringer of justice, the people's avenger. But, also like the guillotine, it can become a sadistic entertainment spectacle."

To Taressa, "canceling someone means disengaging from their toxicity in the name of self-care. And being intentional with where I invest my time, attention, and energy. Nobody is harmed by my withdrawal."

But Ana disagrees. Sure, there ought to be consequences for one's actions—"and public boycotts, petitions, and letter-writing campaigns are all reasonable in and of themselves."

But when these actions are taken on a mass scale against people who aren't significant public figures, Ana says, "It becomes a problem."

"I don't think 'cancel culture' helps society improve," Karie says. "It basically ends up like public bullying and does not solve anything. We all make mistakes and none of us are perfect. Feedback can be provided without trying to destroy someone's life."

"I'm not a fan of the idea that people can't grow and change," Coriel contributes. "I think holding people accountable to growing and changing and owning up to mistakes is healthier, harder, and ultimately far more meaningful work."

"It's easier to write people off than it is to stay engaged and dialogue, hold responsible, educate," says Evangeline. "And I think there are reasons for walking away. Boundaries are healthy. But walking away and making it your life's work to discredit and drag someone's reputation are two different things. We will not get free by engaging in cancel culture."

Clementine Morrigan, a longtime essayist writing about culture, politics, sexuality, and trauma, would agree. "Cancel culture doesn't help abusive people transform their behavior," Morrigan asserts. "Rather, it strips people of what they need to transform their lives. It traumatizes, shames, isolates, and cuts folks off from their material support, which compounds issues leading them to abuse."

She should know. In 2020, Morrigan was "canceled."

"I was truly canceled for no reason," she explains on a recent Instagram post. "I didn't 'say something stupid' or hurt anyone or 'make a mistake.' I didn't do anything." Morrigan was publicly accused of, in her words, "not caring about Black Lives Matter. I contacted the person to say I had been sharing about BLM and that this was clearly visible on my Instagram." When it was demanded that she deplatform, aka, give away her Instagram account, Morrigan stopped engaging.

After this exchange, Morrigan says, "I was called a racist and white supremacist all over the internet. The accusation became that I had been called out for racist behavior and refused to be held accountable.

"I lost almost all my friends," Morrigan further reflected in a 2022 interview on the *Tangle* podcast. Her friends and partners were pressured to "hold her accountable" or "cut ties," Morrigan says, and she was compelled to move from the queer collective house she lived in at the time. "I was called horrible things and totally demonized and misrepresented on a massive scale."

Throughout it all, she refused to apologize or claim innocence. Instead, Morrigan became an outspoken critic of cancel culture and a proponent of building solidarity across difference. She continues to speak and write prolifically and is a cocreator of the *Fucking Cancelled* podcast, which looks at cancel culture through the lens of twelve-step recovery and trauma-reparative justice.

At a recent speaking event in Chicago, Morrigan reflected further on her belief that a person's right to not be slandered or harassed needn't be based on moral purity. "My right to not be humiliated and degraded is not about me being a perfect person who's never done anything wrong in my life," Morrigan said. "If you stay in your integrity and insist on your own humanity, you will find your people."

What We Gain When All Is Lost

When society turns its back on you, it is very difficult to not turn your back on society. Can you ever really trust again? Can you trust the media and the same institutions that have discredited and vilified you?

Lorena Gallo—formerly Lorena Bobbitt—would say yes. Gallo has worked to take control of her own story and redirect the media attention away from her scandal and onto the issue of domestic violence.

"At first it was very difficult," Gallo told NPR's Brooke Gladstone in an episode of *On the Media*. "But since I've been an advocate against domestic violence, listening to the stories of survivors, the victims who are trying to leave but they're not there yet—that gives me strength."

After working with survivors and finding the courage to tell her story, she partnered with filmmaker Joshua Rofé to produce *Lorena*, a four-part docuseries about the events of 1993. Having told her story on her own terms, Gallo says, "I didn't mind the jokes anymore. As long as I shine the light on domestic abuse and make an awareness against domestic violence, then my mission is a noble mission."

Gallo says she feels pride in how she handled it. "I didn't let that or anybody or even John, define who I am."

Similarly, Sydney says she looks back at what she's gone through and feels astonished. "I don't feel proud of everything I said during that time or every way I behaved or anything like that, but I feel proud that I was able to get through it.

"Just to be able to survive something like that feels—" Sydney pauses. "It almost feels like a different person, because I'm like, How did I even? It's kind of unbelievable that I was able to get through all of that."

I know exactly what she means. I look back at who I was then, and all I endured, in astonishment.

"Was it worth it?" I ask Sydney—just as I asked myself for years.

She pauses, takes a deep breath. She talks a little about how Anthony never got what was coming to him, and how what she experienced was a lot worse. After more than a decade, she says, she still feels repercussions. She talks a little about how she is considering changing her last name to further distance herself from those events.

Ultimately, she says, yes. It was worth it.

"I was living a very inauthentic life before," says Sydney. "You know, most of my friends didn't know I was a sex worker already. I was kind of in denial about it myself. I don't think I was, like, living a very authentic, true life at all. And I think this forced me to be way more honest, way more real. I think I'm much more vulnerable in my friendships than I was ever able to be before."

Maligned Women Are Having a Moment—or Are They?

For the last decade, modern-day jezebels from our youth are being resurrected, reexamined, and represented in a more sympathetic light. In documentaries, on podcasts, and in print, audiences are rehashing their stories to help better understand their media treatment and, perhaps, to contend with our own bad behavior. We're exploring the nuance in the situation we may have overlooked at the time, and acknowledging the ways these women were victims, and further victimized by our culture of shame. We're coming to terms with the fact that some of them were more guilty of "whorish" behavior than actual crimes.

In some cases, these women are being handed the mic (see Monica Lewinsky's and Amanda Knox's TED and TEDx Talks). But more often, the same media companies that exploited them years ago continue to profit, editing their words and shaping their image (consider Tonya Harding's less-than-glowing 2018 write-up in the *New York Times*, "Tonya Harding Would Like Her Apology Now"). And some women are being left out entirely. (Has anyone offered Sydney Leathers the sort of softly lit, redemptive profile bestowed upon Theranos CEO Elizabeth Holmes?)

Most unsettling, we're ignoring when the so-called protagonists of such productions object to the content being made. In 1995, Pamela Anderson became the first victim of revenge porn, when a video of her and her then-husband having sex went viral. Speaking of the incident in 2023 to the *Hollywood Reporter*, Anderson says, "I blocked that out of my life. I had to in order to survive, really. It was a survival mechanism.

"Now that it's all coming up again," she says, referring to the Hulu scripted television miniseries, *Pam and Tommy*, "I feel sick from my whole stomach."

Even sympathetic retellings of these stories can do damage to the protagonists. *Framing Britney Spears* is hailed as a sobering examination of the toxic nature of celebrity culture, revisiting a lifetime of gratuitous and misogynistic treatment by the media and paparazzi, including Spears's highly publicized breakdown in 2007. At the end of the documentary, filmmakers note that Spears was asked to be interviewed, but it was "unclear if she received the requests," and so they just plowed ahead.

"I didn't watch the documentary but from what I did see of it I was embarrassed by the light they put me in," Spears later wrote on an Instagram post.

The documentary rehashes the circumstances that led to a California court placing Britney Spears under conservatorship in 2008, granting the twenty-six-year-old's father, Jamie Spears, control of her financial and business affairs, as well as all of her medical and personal decisions. "At a Los Angeles County Superior Court hearing in 2021, Spears told the judge she was medicated against her will, forced to work, and denied basic rights such as getting married, having another child, and even driving her own car," writes Barr & Douds Attorneys, a California law firm that specializes in conservatorship.

After listening to her compelling testimony, more than one million tweets were posted about Britney's conservatorship in just twenty-four hours, including tweets from celebrity supporters like Keke Palmer, Khloé Kardashian, Halsey, Mariah Carey, Madonna, and Cher, to name just a few. ("I feel physically sick about this Britney Spears news," Meghan McCain said in a Tweet. "We as a society have utterly failed her and her dad should be in jail.") Perhaps influenced by public opinion, the court terminated the conservatorship after nearly fourteen years. In 2023, with the release of her book *The Woman in Me*, Britney finally had the opportunity to tell her whole story, on her terms. The book was a bestseller and praised by critics.

Audiences are atoning for our sins, even as we create new victims. We dismiss our indulging in the latest celebrity gossip as a guilty pleasure, defending our nosiness as human nature. Meanwhile, we hold close our own cards, carefully concealing what we fear could make us vulnerable to judgment. Sure, your greatest embarrassment *probably* won't make front page headlines—but what if it did? You won't have a nipple slip at the Super Bowl, but chances are, sooner or later, you will slip up. Our lives are all just as complicated. We are equally imperfect. Sooner or later, you'll express an unpopular opinion, reveal something unseemly, or make a mistake. Then what?

Women, so much more than men, still feel shame, and until we acknowledge that, and why, we will continue to be its victims. And we will continue to victimize others. Make no mistake: this is violence, and it is traumatic—not just for the targets of media humiliation but for everyone involved.

We can no longer stand by, silently, as other women are thrown to the dogs.

"I have never felt more removed from my own humanity," Amber Heard said of the backlash in the *Hollywood Reporter*. "I felt less than a human."

We all know just how that feels.

It is time we start acting that way.

4

Flee, Fight, Fawn, and Freeze

How Women Try (and Fail) to Avoid Shame

"Do you know what happened to the dishwasher?"

It's a simple question, but shame makes even a simple question feel impossible to answer.

The answer is yes. The dishes weren't getting clean, so you took out the bottom rack and unscrewed something, looking for some kind of trap to clean—which you found and cleaned out. But then you couldn't get the bottom piece to screw back in, so you just sort of left it there.

Too long, didn't read: you broke it, and then you didn't want to deal with what you'd done, so you walked away.

You look over at your husband. He's not staring you down in anticipation of a confession. He's just looking at you with a confused, quizzical expression on his face. He's got no clue what you did. Your attempt, and failure, to fix the dishwasher isn't on his radar. He might be momentarily frustrated if you told him, but he wouldn't be seriously angry or anything. But for some reason, waves of shame wash over you. *I can't do anything right. I can't finish anything I start. I'm so bad when it comes to anything technical. I'm such a girl. This is obviously a fundamental character flaw. I'm a terrible person. My husband will hate me.*

I hate myself.

And so, instead of simply fessing up, you make it worse. Do I know what happened to the dishwasher?

"Nope." You frown, shrug, and shake your head for extra emphasis. "No idea," you add unnecessarily, and then it's over.

Except it's not.

Some minutes later you find yourself upstairs, hiding out in your bedroom, folding clothes, ruminating over what you've just done.

Your first, most primal instinct is to blame your husband. Somehow it's his fault, and after a certain amount of mental acrobatics, you figure out how. *This whole thing started when I unloaded the dishwasher and found that the dishes weren't clean. Just why am I having to unload the dishwasher anyway?*

Oh, and to be sure, it's his fault you had to lie. He would have been annoyed with you, and he would have expressed that annoyance. Which would have been . . . annoying. You lied to avoid a fight.

And now you're a liar.

I lied to my husband. Your legs go weak.

Shame has entered the group chat.

Let's Talk About Triggers

Everyone's got certain things that provoke them. For me, any insinuation that I am or might be perceived as a *liar* sets me off. It's what they call a "shame trigger."

Shame gets triggered seemingly out of nowhere. You mention to a coworker that you've been suffering from migraines, and she asks if you've tried losing weight (because you're *fat*). When you ask your Facebook foraging group if it's safe to eat the mushrooms you found in your back garden, the laugh emojis and angry faces come pouring in. Don't you know that mushrooms can kill you (you *moron!*), and so you definitely shouldn't be asking a random Facebook group for an ID (but seriously, how could anyone be so *dumb*)?

Let's look at what, exactly, makes something shameful:

- It's *individualized*. (I'm the only one who can't get on top of my messy house.)
- It's *pathologized*. (Something must be wrong with me that I can't keep this house clean like the beautiful kitchens I see on Instagram.)
- That shame is *reinforced*. (I was already feeling self-conscious about my home and then my sister-in-law offered up a snide comment about my dusty baseboards.)

Of course you can't keep on top of all the laundry when you have a full-time job (and why is doing the household laundry your sole responsibility, anyway?). And actually, lots of people struggle to keep up with housework, especially after they have kids. And most people agree that it's not kind or okay to criticize someone's home—if your houseguest can't get past the sight of a cobweb, that's definitely their problem, not yours. All this is normal, but what is normal versus what is deviant becomes impossible to differentiate when we're in shame's grip.

Shame relates to unwanted and desirable identities—how we do or don't want to be seen. No woman I know, for example, wants to be a *nag*—because nagging is seen as an individual behavior, a personal flaw, instead of a perfectly rational reaction to systemic inequities in the home and workplace and an understandable expression of frustration with the unsustainable burden.

That word, "nag," is just one of a heap of unwanted identities reserved exclusively for women: "airhead," "bag," "bat," "bimbo," "borderline," "bossy," "butterface," "catty," "cat lady," "frigid," "gold digger," "hag," "harpy," "hoe," "horseface," "mannish," "nasty," "priss," "slut," "shopaholic," "tramp," and "trophy wife" are just a few more. Can you even imagine a man being called any of these things?

Regardless of gender, most people hope that others perceive them as being "hardworking," "thoughtful," "positive," "generous," and "kind." We wouldn't like it if we thought people considered us "irresponsible," "lazy," "disorganized," or "dishonest." The characteristics I just listed aren't gendered, but gender and other identities add another dimension. Consider a 2014 study for *Fortune* that examined 248 job reviews of 180 people, 105 men and 75 women. One word appeared seventeen times in women's reviews but never for men: "abrasive." Men were praised for being "assertive," whereas women were admonished for being "bossy," "strident," "irrational," and "aggressive."

An angry man is one thing, but an angry woman? She's a *bitch*. And an angry Black woman? Because society persistently characterizes Black women in particular as ill-tempered, illogical, overbearing, and hostile, "angry" as an identifier becomes even more charged.

A few months ago, a woman in a Facebook group for singles told Shannon she was "selfish" for getting food delivery for just herself, "because the driver won't get as many tips and has to travel a far distance just for one person," Shannon explains.

"While her comment was of course ridiculous, it stuck with me," Shannon says.

"I have a tendency to feel irresponsible whenever I order from Uber Eats because food is always cheaper when made at home. Even if I only order twice a month, both times I will feel ashamed."

Shannon tells me she started to hear that woman's voice whenever she went down to collect her meal.

Upon reflection, Shannon says, "I know where shame comes from: I was raised by a stepdad who insisted that my mom and I not purchase much of anything for ourselves." It also related to societal expectations of her as a single and half-Black woman, Shannon says, as well as the pressure she feels to minimize or hide her disability.

After our conversation, Shannon posted the person's comment on her personal Facebook wall along with her reaction—not to shame the woman who called her selfish, but to overcome the hurt.

"I heard from friends that they, too, order delivery as single people—and I know they're not rich either," Shannon said.

"Some told me I should 'get over it' or 'not pay the person any mind.' That wasn't helpful," Shannon says, "because the voice was there long before the woman reinforced it."

But friends who told her she had the right to order food and that they do the same quieted her internal critical voice.

The Source of Self-Criticism

When you begin to listen to women's stories with an ear toward desirable and unwanted identities, it becomes impossible to miss them.

"I was not planned. I was an *accident*," Kezia says. "My dad had been cheating on his first wife when he met my mom." Maybe for this reason, she continues, "I felt like a *freak* as a child and still do. I identify as a freak. As long as I can remember, I felt different than everyone else." The shame she picked up from others about her origin story still affects the way she thinks about her identity to this day.

Similarly, Annie called herself a "lifelong *outcast*." For Annie, her feelings of exclusion were on account of her physical size. Instead of being "petite, clean, thin, submissive," Annie says, "I'm *big, messy*. I wear size 16 jeans, and I'm *assertive*." Annie claims it's easy to reject a club that never had her as a member to begin with and says she owns her identity as "a middle-aged cat lady," "not cool," and "not fashionable." At the same time, she admits that being physically big remains one of her greatest shame triggers.

This explains Annie's reaction when her husband scolded her for eating four ice cream sandwiches in one sitting. Annie laughs about it now but at the time, she says, it wasn't at all funny. She shut down. Her mind whirred, trying to process what was happening. She became angry and defensive. Her husband's insensitive comment led to a multiday conversation about food choices. In the end, Annie says, "It didn't feel good to feel attacked."

Like Kezia and Annie, Shy recognized at an early age that she would never fit the role that society expected her to inhabit. "I'm a Black queer woman," she explains. But as a child taught to be, as she puts it, "a good, clean, god-fearing, heterosexual Christian," the realization that she was queer "really fucked with me because I doubted whether I was good enough for love and compassion."

Shy was told to ignore hateful opinions, to forgive people, and to "shut them up by proving them wrong," Shy says. "I was told to get thicker skin, otherwise the world is going to chew me up and spit me out."

She tried, but she couldn't shut out the negative comments said to her by members of her family. "I couldn't escape it when I went to school and dealt with the bullying from my peers, or when I walked home and passed older creepy men making inappropriate comments."

At an early age, Shy was already suicidal. "I found no joy in life," she says.

By her twenties, Shy says, "I was ashamed of who I was, where I came from, how I looked—my body, my feet, my face. I mean, I picked apart every part of who I was. I hated myself."

Today, Shy says, "I lean into doing as best as I can, to do and be what feels good to me." As an adult, she has been deliberate about forming relationships with people who share her identity. She also found communities of like-minded people with whom she felt safe, and eventually, as she grew stronger and more confident, she advocated for public acceptance. Speaking out, as we see again and again, is an effective antidote for shame. But it's not always that easy.

What Others Can't Know Hurts Us

For many of us, our shame triggers are complex and multifaceted. We make choices and react to life in the way we do as a result of a lifetime of complex conditioning. Whether you impulsively outed a cheating congressman or accidentally sideswiped another car in the parking lot and drove away, it's not always easy to answer the question "What were you thinking?"

That was certainly the case for me. My choice to become a sex worker was the consequence of innumerable unconscious motivations and latent desires. That, and I needed money.

At the time of my enrollment, Antioch College had what they

called cooperative education—"co-op," for short—a program wherein students alternated academic terms on campus with terms of work or volunteer experience anywhere in the world. I was in Mexico volunteering at a preschool for Indigenous street children. I was nineteen years old. It was my first time out of the States.

I hadn't known what to expect, going to Mexico, only that coming from Ohio—a place so decidedly unromantic—I was sure to find . . . *something*? In a place so far outside the parameters of the familiar, I thought, anything might happen. I could be anyone. On co-op, Antioch's admissions materials had promised, *you can go anywhere.*

The reality of life abroad, as one would imagine, was neither easy nor suddenly romantic. Being that I hadn't chosen a work location from the college's preapproved list, I was responsible for arranging the details of the trip all on my own. Within the first month, my housing fell through. I didn't feel utilized at the charity where I volunteered, and so I stopped going in. Around that same time, I ran out of cash. One day at the grocery store, my credit card was denied. *I guess something's going to have to happen now.*

And then something did. The next afternoon I was on my way to work when I passed a head shop. Before I knew it, I was inside, getting a sloppy butterfly the size of a quarter tattooed on my left shoulder. As the needle drilled in, I told this man my situation. Just as he finished, he asked if I was interested in making some cash. To his mild amusement I said yes.

We met later that evening and, together, took a cab to the club. La Trampa was like a neon flare off the highway in the middle of the night. Something potentially dangerous and thrilling was just what I felt I needed. The tattoo was burning, greased-up from Vaseline. It felt like I'd been punched in the shoulder, and I couldn't believe I'd gone through with it. The tattoo artist did all the talking. I stood back and watched. The owner eventually turned to me and asked in Spanish, "Is this what you want to do? Are you sure?"

At the time I thought, *Yes, definitely. Why not?*

When I first started working in the sex industry, I had no sense that my decision would have any real, far-reaching effects on my life. To the contrary, working at La Trampa felt like a solution for nearly all my problems at the time. No longer bored or lonely, my new job remedied the un-belonging I had been experiencing as a foreigner. Beyond this, I felt as if I'd discovered a seemingly unending source of power and autonomy—relating, in part, to my newfound ability to make money, and lots of it, anywhere in the world.

I had no reason to feel ashamed—and I didn't. Not yet, not really. But from the very start, I was haunted by the fear of what people thought—terrified by the threat of disconnection.

Over the past two decades I have met and spoken to hundreds of women in the sex trades, including countless women who didn't internalize the fear and hatred constantly being impressed upon us on account of our work. I've met lots of women, including sex workers, who feel no shame about their sexual histories. Instead, they're terribly embarrassed by the size of their hands. Or the condition of their car. Someone told me their greatest shame was that their father committed suicide before they were born, and I think, *How can you be ashamed of that?* But I knew the answer: everyone's shame triggers are different.

Shortly after I started working at La Trampa, I called my mom from the pay phone across the street. I told her I'd found a job babysitting. I talked on and on about how well it paid. *I mean really,*

Mom, it's unbelievable. I took funny things that had happened in the club and I changed the setting. I made things up. I lied.

Standing in the glow of the streetlamp, I remember the feeling in my stomach, a sort of charged-up sensation I couldn't name at the time. I had never told a lie of such magnitude to anyone. *But I can never tell her the truth.*

"Whore" is the ultimate unwanted identity. It's a "concealable stigmatized identity," a term that refers to a socially devalued attribute that can be hidden from others. Some obvious examples include LGBTQ+ folks, people with a history of mental illness, and alcohol and drug users (including those in recovery). People who've experienced domestic violence, who are victims of rape or sexual assault, and who've had abortions also make a list, but so do some more unexpected examples: African American homeowners experiencing mortgage strain, for example. Consider a 2015 study published in the *American Journal of Public Health*, which found that upwardly mobile African Americans who had overcome significant structural barriers to buy a home and who were now struggling to pay their mortgage hid their troubles from others to avoid judgment. This concealment led to isolation and contributed to poor mental health outcomes, researchers said.

For some people, a concealable stigmatized identity is just one small, even insignificant, part of the self. But for others, it encompasses a large part of who we think we are, overshadowing other identities and consuming many hours of thought. Internalized stigma, along with discrimination—both experienced and anticipated—can become a considerable source of depression, anxiety, and stress.

"When I was a teen mom and a young single mother, I got the feeling that people expected me to fail at life or to be a statistic,"

Prudence says. "And if I had to guess, many teenaged mothers do find it hard to find their footing in life, especially without a financially and emotionally supportive family.

"From what I can glean, I've surpassed expectations. Even so," Prudence says, "I felt shame around that because I knew people were judging me."

Now in her forties, Prudence is entirely comfortable telling people she had children when she herself was just a teenager, but this wasn't always so—and fellow former teen mom Georgia still feels reticent: "I feel like people are always looking at me like I committed a crime because I had my daughter so young."

For this reason, Georgia keeps her identity as a former teen mom private, obscuring details of her life so others can't find out. For example, Georgia says, "I don't like people asking me my age, because then comes, 'Oh my goodness you have an eighteen-year-old.'"

Eileen says that as a "relinquishing mother"—that is, a person who has given a child up for adoption—"I am not considered a 'real mother.' I feel the pressure to 'move on' and 'stop living in the past.' Truth is, that kind of trauma—separation from a much-loved and wanted child—is a daily reality that gets worse over time."

As a result of society's misconceptions, Eileen tells me she is less forthcoming than she used to be. "I answer in single word answers," she says. "'Do you have any children?' 'Yup, a son.' Period."

"Now, everyone knows, but I lied to 99 percent of the people I knew about my entire childhood," Lara says. "I didn't want them to know that I grew up in the foster system.

"Nobody wants their son to marry a woman who was in foster care," Lara says. "She couldn't possibly be a good parent herself. She couldn't possibly be healthy."

Lara lied to protect herself from that stigma, she says, and "to hopefully open doors that others inherently had easy access to—and it actually worked. I developed a social circle of nice people from nice backgrounds who referenced me for nice jobs and I moved into a nice, safe life.

"At the same time," Lara says, "I felt like an inauthentic person and I felt very guilty about it, and I had a deep feeling of loneliness because I was not having honest relationships with many people. I kept my distance, emotionally, and that was very hard for me. I loved many of those people, and I was dishonest with them. I'm not great at lying, so it took a toll on me."

The Four Responses to Shame

Right about now you may be thinking, *Just don't let it get to you. Conquer your shame. Overcome your triggers. Who cares what people think?*

The answer is that we all care, deeply. We are hardwired for connection. Love and belonging are irreducible needs. The absence of love leads to suffering, and experts say that feeling safe with other people is the single most important aspect of mental health.

Rafts of studies have identified social support as one of the most consistent predictors of post-traumatic growth—that is, our ability to experience a positive psychological change after surviving a traumatic or stressful life event.

Shame, however, can disrupt our ability to access this kind of vital social support just when we need it most. At the neural level, shame is associated with the amygdala, the part of the brain designed to keep us safe from threats, activating the sympathetic nervous system and generating the flight/fight/fawn/freeze response. In a misguided effort to protect ourselves from danger, we involuntarily push away the family, friends, and community who might just be there to support us (if only we'd give them a chance). Gerald Fishkin, practicing psychotherapist and author of *The Science of Shame and Its Treatment*, describes shame as "the ghost in the machine of the human mind," a supernatural force wreaking havoc on a person's self-worth and behavior. Remember: shame makes us fear others, perceiving them as the threat. Understanding this deep-seated fear and how it unconsciously motivates our behavior—and figuring out how to circumvent the knee-jerk reactions that work against our own best interests—is the key to restoring our sense of worth.

Flee

The flight response involves a release of hormones that signal your body to run from the danger or threat. When you flee, you literally or metaphorically isolate yourself and hide from the perceived threat. If you're about to be attacked by an animal, it makes a lot of sense to turn on your heels and run as fast as you can. But when you're feeling attacked by your shaming mother-in-law, this instinct may not serve you quite as well.

Here are a couple of situations that illustrate the kind of panicked, avoidant behavior we'd characterize as fleeing:

My sister shames me that my son didn't go to college and isn't where she thinks he should be in life. I feel shame about my mothering and worry that I didn't handle things right as he was growing up. I can feel myself deflate. I can't look up. I sink down into myself and try and change the subject.

I was bartending at a restaurant and I was running late. My hair was up and my makeup wasn't done. Before I could go in the bathroom and make myself presentable, the manager came over, looked me dead in the eye, and goes, "You shouldn't have even come in. You look like shit." My stomach sunk. I felt worthless. I felt so embarrassed. I finished my shift, and I never went back.

I remember being six or seven years old and having a swim instructor at our local pool make fun of my "boobs." That was the first time that I can remember being ashamed of my body and it hurt even more because he was someone that I looked up to. I wore a T-shirt whenever swimming for the next decade or so.

From the start, I avoided thinking too deeply about the choices I was making, including my decision to lie. By not telling my mom— or my boyfriend, Rick—I thought I could escape judgment and shame. It was a classic example of flight.

Two or three weeks after I'd started working there, La Trampa took me off the schedule. They told me it was because I was working illegally. I took it as a rejection and immediately looked for another club willing to hire me. For the next couple weeks, I made the rounds among a couple of the lesser strip clubs. None of them were as nice as La Trampa, and one or two were downright dangerous. These clubs lacked security. The dressing rooms weren't monitored. There was no one to walk you out at the end of your shift. You left out the same exit as the last customers, the drunkest and most desperate, and you got into the back seat of the first taxi that stopped.

After all that, I was ready to go home. I used the money I earned to buy my mom a plane ticket to visit me during my last week in Mexico. It was her first time out of the States. We spent the time exploring Oaxaca as tourists, and then we flew home together, back to Ohio.

Driving home from the airport, everything looked the same. It was early April. Patches of winter's last snow still mottled the front lawns of our suburban streets. Everything here was still the same, I remember thinking, except me. I was different. The world, I had learned, was bigger than these small houses and the small minds they contained.

I felt superior—and then I looked at my mother and I felt guilty.

Keys still swaying in the ignition, she asked me how it felt to be home.

"Different," I said.

"You must have stories—things you still haven't told me."

"Not really."

"Yeah, right," my mom said, not lightly. Then, "Maybe, someday, you'll tell me the good stuff, too."

I remember in this moment, feeling overcome by panic, desperate for an exit. I would never tell my mom the "good stuff," I remember thinking. *She would never understand.*

Fleeing happens in many ways. I physically left Mexico to try to leave my actions and my shame behind. And here is where many of the avoidant behaviors began. From drinking and smoking pot to excessively exercising, overworking, and overspending money on frivolous things, I've tried nearly everything to run from my negative feelings.

To avoid shame, Kezia says, "I drink too much. I engage in risky behaviors. I stop talking to people I care about."

"Sometimes," N'Kenge admits, "to prove (to myself, mostly) that I'm not poor anymore, I overspend."

"At my best," Eileen says, "I get away from the stressor. I freewrite or go for a brisk walk. At my worst, I fall into binge-watching movies or TV. I reach for a stiff drink."

For Vicki, as for many women, attempts to evade shame masquerade as self-improvement.

"I can't remember a time when I wasn't dieting," she tells me. "Ever since I was around ten years old, when my mother told me I looked like a sausage in my tight, tight pants."

Vicki says, "I was always looking for a diet. I was counting the calories, I was writing down the food I ate. Here's my goal for the day or week, did I meet it? Always a goal. Did I exercise? I measured my thighs and arms with a tape measure. I was totally into it! It was all tied to a belief that one day I'm going to achieve this thing: I'm going to look perfect and attract a man."

One day in the high school bathroom, Vicki and her friends taught one another how to purge. When she realized the relief that came with puking, Vicki says, "I got hooked. It was like drinking. It made me feel drunk."

From that day on, Vicki says, she would binge and purge "and there were no ramifications! Sure," she says with a laugh, "I had bloodshot eyes, my face would get puffy, and thirty years later my teeth are cracking off—it caught up to me. But I could stop dieting."

In retrospect, Vicki says, "It was all about self-hate. I hated my skin. It was all from the sexual abuse, thinking that if I became the right shape or size, [it] would make that feeling go away."

These days, there's a saying I remind myself of when I've over-come by shame: "Don't just do something, sit there." As in, sit there and be present with the feelings you may desperately want to avoid. Of course, we all know how hard that can be. When in shame, it may feel difficult to sit still, stay in a room, or even speak. Keeping ourselves quiet or excusing ourselves from the situation seems safer than the alternative. As my one friend put it, "I either shrink myself, get quiet and hide, or I turn into a fucking monster and rage."

Fight

In certain situations, however, shame tempts you to move *toward*, rather than away from, the confrontation. Another mom at drop-off looks at your kid and asks if you remembered that it's picture day. Someone online challenges your political viewpoint. A colleague not-so-gently teases you about your smelly lunch. Your face grows hot. Maybe you're already feeling stressed and irritable. Now cortisol and adrenaline are coursing through the body, empowering you to ward off or "fight" the antagonist. Angry outbursts, bullying, and controlling behavior all count as fighting. You might not physically attack your neighbor who confronts you about the bulk trash you let pile up in your driveway, but you're still on the defense.

"For most of my life I've hated my body," Brazen Lee admits. "Fat people are expected to be awkward, lazy, dumb, clumsy, lonely, single, greedy, inactive, incapable, gross, and smelly."

Then there's the body positivity movement, she continues, which "expects me to love myself in spite of constant mockery, shaming, hatred, and abuse."

The internal and external pressure is, Brazen says, "constant, crushing, and ubiquitous."

It's no wonder that rage is her go-to emotion. Her "tantrums," as Brazen calls them, range from eye-rolling or huffing at strangers to raising her voice impatiently to raging out loud. And anyone might be the target: "My roommate, my mom, some dumbass on the bus who is blocking the aisle. The pharmacist on the phone while I stand there waiting, clearly in a hurry."

Anger comes with a surge of adrenaline. "It feels *good*," Brazen says. "Then comes defensiveness. I've learned enough about myself to know that defensiveness usually means I'm in the wrong."

When in shame, we feel neglected, invisible, and slighted. We perceive shame as an attack, and so we fight back.

Shamed by an abusive boss, one friend says, "I felt rage and the need for revenge the next day. I also felt mad at myself because I realized I was *allowing* someone to make me feel that way. How dare I allow that?"

"It definitely feels shameful to be divorced with a child who has a deadbeat father," says Sarina. "Makes me look like I make poor choices, which I clearly sometimes do."

Growing up with a facial disfigurement, Ariel Henley is no stranger to public humiliation. Anger motivated her to become an author and disability rights activist. She's a seasoned professional, but even someone as experienced and resilient as Ariel loses her cool.

A few weeks ago, Ariel says, "a kid at the airport started staring at me and pointed at my face. The child made a comment to his mom asking what was wrong with me. Instead of shutting it down, she laughed and stared with him.

"I didn't handle it well," Ariel admits. "I told the mom that she and her kid were extremely rude, and not only should she know better but she should teach her kid better because that's how kids grow up to be assholes."

Ariel felt ashamed by their reaction to her appearance, she admits, "but I felt more ashamed at my response."

Like Ariel and many of the women I spoke to, Brazen channels her rage into activism.

"For most of my life I've hated my body," Brazen repeats. "But then, about fifteen years ago, I started doing sex work. Suddenly I was making all of this money and banging all of these hot dudes. Me, the girl who never had dates and has never really been in love. I was being paid to have my body worshipped, adored, cared for by (for the most part) beautiful men."

Thanks to working in the sex industry, Lee says, she realized that there were probably many men in her life who were into her but never made any moves out of fear and shame.

"This was a big moment in my life, one when my confidence grew," Brazen says.

Being a sex worker and sex-positive person became central to Brazen's identity—rather than conceal herself she vehemently defends it and her right to trade sex for cash. In a blog post titled "An Open Letter to Anti-Sex Work Activists," Brazen confronts feminists who'd describe that transaction as inherently violent.

"I literally fill up with rage when you refer to me, and folks like me, as 'prostituted women,'" Lee writes. "I am not being 'prostituted' by anyone. I am a free-thinking, independent person who decided, a few years ago, when I got so tired of being unemployed and in constant poverty, to market myself and grow a business around something I enjoyed immensely, and regularly did for free: sex."

Later in the essay she further explains her reasons for selling sex. "It was becoming clear that finding a suitable partner for dating or marriage wasn't going to happen. So I decided to start charging for access to my body. Maybe that sounds sad to you, but this is the reality."

Like so many women with experiences in the sex trades, myself included, Brazen was fighting to reclaim her presumably shameful, unwanted identity and transform it into a positive feature. It's an adaptive strategy—but you can hear unspoken pain underneath her rage.

My first instinct after encountering sex work may have been to flee Mexico, back home to the safety of Ohio. But something kept drawing me back in. I was fighting to figure out who I was and what I wanted. I was fighting with myself. I was fighting in my head with everyone who'd have told me what I was doing was wrong.

That fall after I returned home to the States, Rick and I lived together in Cincinnati, where he was attending classes while I worked nights on call as a hospital advocate for a rape crisis center in nearby Covington, Kentucky. I told myself what happens in Mexico stays in Mexico. But some nagging urge kept pulling me back to stripping. I couldn't have explained why. After some convincing, Rick started letting me drop him off at the lab in the mornings so that I could borrow his car in the afternoons while he was at work. Maybe I told him I was going to the library. Or working days at the shelter. I forget what I told him. I continued to lie.

Forty-five minutes out of Cincinnati, right off I-75, there was a forty-foot dilapidated billboard cartoon of a woman with enormous breasts, black stars for nipples. Leroy's Topless Cabaret: exit 42. Leroy's didn't take itself too seriously, and I liked that. I liked Leroy's because I could come and go as I wanted. I could make money any way that I wanted to. I liked Leroy's because I didn't have to wash my hair for work. I could go in greasy-headed and still make two, three hundred bucks in a four-hour shift.

By now, sex work had become less an act of rebellion and more a means to an end. It was no longer so much about the money as it was that I needed the intangible something I gained from men who paid just to be near me and tell me I was beautiful. I did not stop to examine how or why sex work made me feel powerful, nor interrogate the illusory nature of that control.

At some point in graduate school, I came across the phrase "pride identity" in an obscure case study by a researcher named Olga Sasunkevich. Sasunkevich used the term to describe how Belarusian women involved in "shuttle work" represented themselves and constructed a sense of self in spite of the stigma imposed upon them by their jobs.

Shuttle work involves taking frequent trips to a foreign country to buy goods as cheaply as possible to sell back home for a slightly higher price. It is physically hard work, low profit, and not prestigious, and yet the women Sasunkevich spoke to represented themselves in idealized ways. Even though they experienced ridicule and discrimination, they insisted they were serious, successful, and self-reliant businesswomen—and not to be pitied.

Reading Belarusian market women's struggles to explain and defend their livelihood, I recognized my own absurd fight to save face. In my head, I was warring, constantly, with negative voices, defending myself against other people's hypothetical opinions of my work. Fearful of harshly critical judgments, I sought out individuals and communities that held naively accepting views on sex work, even as other people's ready dismissal of moral judgments did nothing to assuage the negative feelings inside me. In fact, the more people reacted positively to my occupation, the more I felt it necessary to minimize negative on-the-job experiences and deny complicated early life experiences that had influenced my choice.

Fawn

Of the four reactions to shame, fawning is probably the most confusing, baffling, and cringeworthy. It involves making yourself vulnerable to the very thing that's causing you pain. It's approval-seeking, being overly flattering and sycophantic in hopes of keeping yourself safe. Why, if you are so ashamed of something or someone, wouldn't you fight back? Why would you subject yourself to a situation or person repeatedly—even when you don't enjoy it or it's actively undermining your well-being?

Back on campus the next semester at my ultra–liberal arts college, I convinced myself I was an "empowered" sex worker, even though the idea that I was empowered by my occupation as a stripper was not exactly true. For one, I was not what one would call "sex positive." Though I tried to embrace the belief that all consensual sexual activities were fundamentally healthy and pleasurable, that wasn't what I'd been raised to believe, nor was it my experience.

Today, when it comes to individual experiences in the sex trades—what sex workers want and what they need—I am confident in my political positions. But I also readily admit that sex work didn't begin for me as a political statement. I started stripping because I needed the money, and the fact that I enjoyed the work—and wanted to keep doing it long after I "needed" to—only confused me. I felt ashamed of that confusion and ashamed of what everything that I did for money said about me. If only I had been given space to explore and make sense of that confusion.

When I thought of my mom, I felt angry. I felt sad. I felt guilty. I felt trapped, like whatever room I was in was losing its air. I felt panic. Like the walls were coming in on me.

The one thing I knew for sure: she would not approve of what I was doing. When thoughts of her and what she'd say about my work came up, I'd push those thoughts away. I pushed her away, too. I stopped writing and calling as often. When we did speak, I'd say whatever I thought she wanted to hear, fawning all over her to deflect the shame I felt creeping up from behind, a nagging preoccupation that I'd become a disappointment.

In her memoir, *Strung Out*, Erin Khar reflects back on the years she struggled with heroin addiction, including the early weeks of her first pregnancy, a fact the baby's father held over her head for years. "I didn't think I could let go of shame. I didn't think I could tell the truth. I didn't think I could forgive myself or not see myself as a monster." Erin married the man, and they stayed married for years in spite of his repeated infidelities because she feared he'd take away her kid. It was, she says, in a way, a kind of fawning.

Fawning is people-pleasing, codependency, lack of identity or boundaries. We fawn in instances where we don't feel safe and don't feel like we have the power to fight back. We also fawn in moments where a fight just doesn't seem worth it.

When your neighbor calls you "babe," a coworker refashions your ideas as his own, or the man behind the deli counter won't give you your lunch order until you give him a smile, what do you do? Often, we smile, laugh, or superficially agree, anything to placate the perpetrator, even as it leaves us feeling shameful and complicit. This fawning behavior creeps into our lives in so many insidious ways:

I think for a large part of my adult life I have lived shrouded in fear, wanting to accommodate.

As a woman, I think society expects me to do everything for everyone in my family . . . and be perky about it.

Women are supposed to be agreeable and keep everyone around us feeling comfortable . . . a happy, loving, attentive wife and mother—a woman who takes care of others. This is what is expected of me.

I think society wants me to be quiet and timid. I think society wants me to be soft and demure. I am not any of those things until I am challenged, and then I lose all sense of a backbone.

"I like to come off as smart, cool, confident, and put together"— and for the most part Karie does. But when she's afraid she won't be perceived this way, she says, "I usually tone down my Southern accent. I dress a little more professionally. I wait for others to start conversations before chiming in so I don't say anything stupid. I'm careful to read the room before engaging with anyone. I do everything in my power to blend in."

This was me, for years, trying to blend in. If you know me now, you know how absurd this is—I am so obviously not a blend-in kind of gal. But that's what I tried to do. I knew my work as a stripper would not be accepted, and so I hid this truth entirely. I omitted facts and rearranged my narratives. I tried to keep my story as simple as possible so as not to forget some obscure detail and be "found out." But no matter how much I tried to detach myself from my past, it loomed over me until, by the end of it all, I felt held hostage to my own impossible and implausible collection of lies.

I dared to dream that if my mother found out, she might understand. In my wildest fantasies, I thought she might even be proud. Thanks to stripping, I could work and go to school. I could participate in the unpaid internships taken for granted as part of the undergraduate experience. For the first time in my life, I felt financially secure. My coworkers were smart, beautiful, and resilient. I admired them. I wanted to believe my mom would admire them, too, if only she knew.

The next spring, a year after my Mexico study abroad, I found myself overseas again. This time, I was in London, volunteering at an organization that advocated against female genital mutilation. At night, I worked at a table-dancing club called Images. Sometimes Rick would forget the time difference and call in the middle of the night, just as I was returning home from my shift. He was back in Cincinnati, going to a normal college and behaving like a normal college kid, attending classes and frat parties, doing keg stands, playing beer pong, and experiencing all the other ridiculous things that normal students do.

When he'd call he sounded drunk and far away. He'd say things like: Where are you? And why did you go away? And when are you coming home? *He loves me,* I thought. In these moments and for years, I believed that he was flawless. I felt an obligation to protect him, to see that nothing and no one ever hurt him, least of all me. *I will never tell him the truth,* I thought, *about who I am and what I am capable of. What I am,* I thought, *is something of a monster. A liar. A cheat.* I would never tell him the truth, I decided, even if it meant being less than true for the rest of my life.

What, I dared not even ask, was the alternative?

Freeze

Freeze is perhaps the most frightening, and stigmatizing, response to shame. It is similar to but a more extreme version of flight. The freeze response involves completely shutting down, going numb or being "frozen." Like a deer in headlights, your breathing is restricted, your eyes are still, your limbs go heavy, and you cannot move. At its extreme, this response becomes disassociation, which Bessel van der Kolk defined in an interview with Still Harbor as "a temporary putting aside, not knowing, and not noticing. It's a way to survive. Blocking things out allows many traumatized people to go on." Van der Kolk notes that the reaction may be very helpful in the moment, in order to make it through the crisis, "but in the long range, living your life in a dissociative way only keeps the trauma alive."

When we talk about disassociation, we're talking about situations that assault our nervous system with negative feelings so greatly that we completely shut down. Consider the following examples:

My cousin was being bullied by an older relative and two friends to dance on a table. When they told her to remove her underwear, she started to cry. The teens laughed at her, and she ran off. I just froze. I was a year older than my cousin and felt powerless to say anything.

The administration of the last school I worked at judged me heavily for advocating for mental health awareness and being open about my own struggles. They ended up convening a specialized governing board meeting to fire me. I was not allowed to speak or testify on my behalf. This crushed my soul and my confidence. I felt gross. Uncomfortable. I suffered from back pain and had trouble breathing. On really bad days, I couldn't get out of bed or leave the house. To this day, this is embarrassing to me.

After an ex cheated and broke up with me, I went to the house we lived in to pick up my things. When I arrived, he and a group of his friends were all sitting on the porch waiting for me. My belongings were in a pile next to my ex who had the girl he cheated on me with sitting on his lap. I had to walk past all of his friends to get to the pile. As I walked by, they called me fat, slut, bitch, whatever. One of them tripped me. He and the girl were laughing. I don't know how I survived this moment. I went numb.

When it came to sources of shame that can set off the freeze response and disassociation, sex revealed itself as a number one trigger. Multiple women I interviewed said that physical intimacy elicited such strong feelings of inadequacy that, during sex, they'd go numb and just not be present in their bodies, "shut off [their] brain," or think of something else.

"I sometimes feel like I have to force myself to have sex," one friend shared when asked to reflect on a present-day shame she grapples with, adding that years of therapy and "really getting into my younger days" actually made finding pleasure from physical intimacy more difficult.

"I struggle to stay present during sex with my husband," another said. "The shame comes when I think it's a reflection on our marriage—when, really, I know it's due to past trauma." A search of the keyword "sex" in a Facebook group for marriage and long-term partnership support shows how widespread the problem is.

"I have, over the years, almost completely lost my sex drive to the point where I genuinely wouldn't mind never having sex again," one woman writes, adding, "I feel so terrible about this."

"Having sex feels like marriage maintenance at this point for me," another commiserates. "I blame my body insecurities . . . parts that used to feel sexual now feel totally utilitarian and unattractive, and I don't really desire for them to be seen or touched. Of course we're exhausted from young kids, but it's hard to imagine this ever changing."

Even when sex was physically painful, women said they felt obligated to perform, and ashamed of their lack of desire. For their partners' sakes, they would "give in" or "suffer through it." Some women admitted they'd pretend to find sex pleasurable, but others said they can't or won't. ("I used to pretend but now I don't even want to bother. I have literally scrolled Facebook or played Candy Crush while having sex.")

Stories like this would come to no surprise to writer and therapist Kerry Cohen, who theorizes that for women, sex is trauma, performance, or intimacy. "Almost every woman I know has a complicated relationship to sex," she wrote in a piece for *Psychology Today*.

Sex and giving birth, Cohen says, are two of the most vulnerable experiences a body can go through. No wonder motherhood also emerged as a major pain point and source of shame that can trigger the freeze response and disassociation.

"No one tells you how exhausting, and degrading, it can feel to breastfeed," one friend shares. "I lie in bed after she's gone to sleep just trying to return to my body."

Many women who breastfeed, and even moms who don't, can become "touched out"—that is, they feel an overwhelming discomfort and aversion toward any more physical contact. Being touched out is a type of sensory overload. It is also associated with a loss of bodily autonomy and brings up questions and issues surrounding consent. On the *What Fresh Hell* podcast, Amanda Montei, author of *Touched Out: Motherhood, Misogyny, Consent, and Control*, describes it as the shameful feeling that your body has become "like a toy, a snot rag, just this thing to be used and trampled on."

> To have your body tugged at constantly, to have your naked body stared at by your children, especially if those things have happened before, experiences with men or other sexual partners in ways that left a mark, or caused you to feel like your sense of autonomy or consent were violated . . . all that unresolved stuff tends to, or can, really bubble up.

These things are incredibly difficult to talk about. But not talking about something only makes it exponentially worse. To be sure, that was my experience. If only I had told the truth about my job from the beginning, I lamented. Now it was too late. My lies had built a cage around me and I sat in it, wanting to be free so badly that I just pretended that I was.

Then, one afternoon, I was sitting at my desk at my day job when I got an email from my mother. Subject: your dancing.

She said she was humiliated. "I know you're stripping," she said. "I am not a stupid or naive woman." "This is all my fault," it went on. "If I hadn't been broke on my ass all the time and able to give you adequate spending money, none of this would've happened." She compared my having lied about my job to my father's adultery. She said it made her want to puke.

Who knows how long I sat there, lingering over the words. Time slowed down. My rational mind abandoned me. I had waited and imagined this moment for so long. And in many ways, it was so much worse than I feared. I froze.

Whereas a supportive response would have mitigated the impact of my experiences in the industry, my mother's response to the discovery that I was stripping was hostile, negative, and shaming. Her rejection tapped into deep-seated childhood fears that I was unlovable. The fear, distrust, and isolation I had already begun to experience as an individual working in the sex industry was compounded. My sense of self was shattered—my sense of trust in my mother, destroyed.

At the time I pushed the thought of all this away. I needed to believe she still loved me. That I was lovable. In spite of what I'd become.

I wrote her back immediately and I told her she didn't have to worry. I was an adult, I said. I was capable of making decisions for myself. I told her I was glad that she'd figured it out, actually, because now I could start paying my own way for things—which I did. I paid off my credit card; I started paying my own tuition. And I bought her a plane ticket to come visit me in Europe. That's right, I totally fawned.

That spring, my mother and I traveled together all through Amsterdam, Paris, Barcelona—we went everywhere, money no concern. I paid for everything, obviously. I spared no expense. I had hoped we'd have fun, but it wasn't fun at all. Something felt wrong and the feeling couldn't be shaken. Every time I paid for something—a meal, a hotel room, a souvenir—we both knew where that money was coming from, but neither of us spoke of it. When she went back to the States, I felt lonelier than ever.

Becoming the Witness We Deserved

Flee, fight, fawn, or freeze—we often have a tendency toward one of these reactions to shame, but like me you've probably cycled through all of them in your lifetime. The key is to start to recognize your own shame trigger, understand your knee-jerk response, and then take steps to unwind that reaction and find a different way forward. One way I've found is retelling and reclaiming our own stories.

It's a lesson that's hard to learn. After all, we've spent so much of our lives keeping these so-called shameful secrets to ourselves.

"I do keep some things hidden," Annie admits. "Like, I've never told my husband how many people I've slept with. He has no idea. I don't know the exact number myself, but it's somewhere around a hundred.

"I will never tell him my number of partners because I don't think he's capable of handling that kind of information," Annie says. "And it would make him look at me in a different light."

Pamela grew up in a quaint, conservative suburb less than an hour north of New York City. Upper middle-class community. Catholic private schools, Italian American family. "I just really never had to be concerned about where my next meal was coming from or what clothes I could wear. At Christmas there were always, like, a ton of presents. We took vacations frequently."

Pamela's father was the first in his family to go to college. He went to medical school and became a doctor. "I think they felt really proud that they were able to make this life for themselves." But coming from a privileged background, Pamela says, "I felt a ton of shame. From a young age, I was always apologizing to service people.

"She's a good student. She's a good girl, she listens to rules," Pamela says of her younger self. "I was really obedient. I was really polite." On the inside, she says, "I was angry all the time."

Around the age of eight, Pamela started exhibiting symptoms of obsessive-compulsive disorder, or OCD. "I washed my hands a lot, until they would bleed. It was really confusing to me, because obviously if you're young and you're having this happen to you for the first time, you have no idea what's really going on."

When she went to her parents for help, "It was pretty quickly shut down. It was overlooked or dismissed as a phase or a dramatic moment."

The attitude that OCD is unserious was reinforced by society. "OCD is a disease everyone downplays," Pamela says. "People are just like, oh, it means you're clean. If you've seen my house, I'm not a neat person. I don't order things around. Instead, I have a shit ton of intrusive thoughts that make me feel like a monster."

As Pamela says, "Grade school is always just like a nightmare any-way" but for her, untreated OCD meant constant rumination, desperate attempts to deflect any negative attention, and having to navigate it all without support.

To get by, Pamela imitated the popular kids. She wore sports clothes and pretended to like rap. By eighth grade, she went in the opposite direction, listening to Nirvana and dressing in flannels and torn jeans. She started reading poetry and became, as she calls it, a "Plath girl." Even though it got her made fun of, to Pamela, this identity felt more authentic.

Pamela met Dave at a literary event. He was a poet and interested in the things she was interested in. Pamela says, "I felt lucky. But it got dark real fast."

One evening early in the relationship, Dave and Pamela had sex. "When I did not want to sleep with him a second time that night, he punched the wall.

"I was terrified. My whole body"—Pamela brings her arms up in front of her chest and clenches her fists—"I thought if he could see that I was afraid, he would stop. Obviously, that's not what happened."

They dated for another eight months.

"Then he broke up with me, which is another kind of . . . real embarrassing. People are like, how did you escape? And I'm like, well, actually, he dumped me."

Pamela tried to move on, just as she did when her parents rejected her bid for support. Two years later, she was in a healthy relationship and working toward a PhD when, she says, "I totally fucking lost my shit.

"I was reading and studying and teaching a few classes and just feeling like a total failure at everything. The OCD, and anxiety, and I had insomnia. I had stopped sleeping. I was suicidal."

Pamela came clean, she says, because she didn't want to die. And because she knew that she could trust her boyfriend.

"I called Steve, and I said, You need to come home from work now because I'm in your apartment and I can't leave and I'm going to die. And I need to go to a hospital."

Steve called his cousin, a psychologist at Columbia Presbyterian Hospital on the Upper West Side "and I called my dad," Pamela says. "Because my mom wasn't picking up the phone. I said, Dad, I'm gonna die. You need to drive me to this hospital. And I'm sorry."

The hospital admitted Pamela, and she stayed overnight.

"The next day I went home and I was like, 'Is this it? Because I'm not better!'"

And so she went back to the hospital that afternoon.

"They were like, you look great. And I literally was going to tell them I'm fine. And then I went out and Steve was like, you need to go back in there and cry and you need to tell them you need to stay."

Pamela was hospitalized for a week. "They put me on the right medication and set me up with a therapist."

Now forty years old, the disorder shifts and changes over time, she says, and is dependent on the stress. "I've been in therapy for, you know, fifteen years now and on medication. So that really helps."

When it comes to the hospitalization, Pamela says, she never felt ashamed. "It felt liberating, it felt like, fucking finally. The shit was coming to the surface." Even after others had failed her, even after she'd failed herself, she didn't give up.

"One of the scariest—but ultimately most liberating things—I've ever done was let go of my denial," Jennifer Pastiloff writes on Instagram. "May you remember the freedom that comes with telling yourself the truth is worth the temporary cost of fear and discomfort."

I remember. I will never forget. The memory of what I've lived through and survived spurs me on. It inspires my activism. It leads me through my daily life, one choice to the next. I did not, as some anonymous Instagram post once said, crawl through the shards of my own brokenness to live a mediocre life. My life today is beyond whatever feeble dreams I held for myself for all those years that I was suffering, and I am so grateful to "past me" for doing the work.

"I have so much love and empathy for my younger self," Pamela says. "I feel like she was struggling so much. Even though you had everything, you had nobody. And that sucks. You felt so alone. And you felt like no one was listening to you. But I heard you, and I love you."

Making connections, experts say, is our saving grace. Meaningful connections heal nervous system dysregulation and restore limbic resonance, which is what happens when you and another person are fully absorbed in conversation, sitting face-to-face, and meeting each other's gaze. It works best when you look into each other's eyes, but I'd argue it can happen virtually, too. Limbic resonance is the opposite of shame. It's a feeling of being completely seen, heard, and understood. It's how I felt when I first listened to Pamela tell her story. It is how I feel each time I reread it. My whole nervous system relaxes. Perhaps, reading these stories, you feel it, too.

It's hard work, but healing from shame is possible. As the poet Rainer Maria Rilke so eloquently wrote, "Let everything happen to you: beauty and terror. / Just keep going. No feeling is final."

Part 2

Overcoming Shame

5

Only as Sick as Our Secrets

Oversharing as a Feminist Act

The first day of class, a dozen or so of us huddled expectantly around a folding table in a common space at St. Mark's Church-in-the-Bowery. Terrified of what people might think, until this moment, I had kept my experience—and my writing—mostly to myself.

Then Larry Fagin entered like a beatnik hummingbird in his old-white-man-poet costume of a black turtleneck and jeans, his Reebok sneakers squeaking as he darted around us. The lecture was digressive, tangential—it was less a lecture, it seemed, than performance art. He was the authority in the room, I believed, simply because he'd said so.

At one point, he interrupted himself and burst into a jazz riff that went on for at least two or three minutes. As it continued, I shot a look around the room but no one returned my irritated disbelief.

The fact that everyone else seemed to get it, and I just didn't . . . well, that shut me right up.

The rest of the evening I laughed only when I felt I was supposed to; mostly, I nodded appreciatively on cue.

I was the problem, I decided. It was me. I was *basic*. Norah Jones. She was popular at the time, a fact that seemed to infuriate Fagin.

Halfway through that first class, he went off on a rant condemning the multi-Grammy-winning singer-songwriter for her mediocrity. The more he dug into Norah Jones for being boring, the more it felt as if he were talking about me. A wide-eyed Midwesterner relatively new to New York, I had a full-time job at a nonprofit and lived with my high school sweetheart in an overpriced cookie-cutter apartment on Manhattan's Lower East Side. Despite my provocative past, I had settled into a decidedly normal life. Not an artist's life, I sometimes feared.

Older, male, interesting, untethered to the rules of syntax or society—a poet—Larry Fagin was everything I was not. By the end of that first class, I was desperate to impress him.

Coming over to his apartment one night for a private session was part of the deal. Larry Fagin occupied two rent-controlled apartments on the Lower East Side, one the disheveled quarters you might expect of a then-sixtysomething-year-old bachelor, the other filled to the brim with books. When he offered me the last glass of a bottle of wine, I saw my manuscript on the table.

I don't remember a lot about the feedback other than all the red ink. He criticized the work as overly descriptive and sentimental, slashing away figurative language until barely any text was left. What I'd hoped would be affecting prose, Fagin dismissed as affected. Certainly, I lacked control over my manuscript. According to Fagin, what I lacked was talent.

"What should I do?" I asked, seeing no options other than to give up.

"Quit your day job!" Fagin nearly shouted. "Leave your boyfriend! Lower your expenses! Devote yourself to your craft!"

Fagin waved off my plans to apply to an MFA program, saying the workshop model only made bad writing worse. Then he suggested that I work with him privately instead, somehow suggesting I pay for it with sex.

I don't remember exactly how he phrased it, even as I remember so many other details distinctly. I remember the red stain around his lips and how his breath smelled of wine. I told myself he was drunk and that he didn't know what he was doing. I might've played it off like he was joking, although he definitely wasn't, or maybe I just said no. Certainly, I minimized what happened. I blamed myself.

Today I know that regardless of whether or not we've had sex for money, and regardless of what we choose to write or speak about, some men will never see women—whether we are writers, lawyers, doctors, astronauts, or sex workers—as anything other than whores. But at the time, I believed that with the content of my work, I had invited the proposition.

I had not yet paid the enrollment fee and so for that reason it was easy to drop out, but for other reasons the decision felt difficult. It felt like I was failing, accepting defeat. I fought with myself over the decision, but ultimately, I fled.

In a 2013 op-ed for the *New York Times*, Joyce Maynard describes herself at eighteen, the year she took up an affair with J. D. Salinger, as "a young person in possession of particular vulnerabilities as well as strengths."

Years after he dismissed her, Maynard writes, "his voice stayed in my head, offering opinions on everything he loved and all that he condemned. This was true even though, on his list of the condemned, was my own self."

What an accurate description for us all.

But here's what we can all do to reclaim ourselves and banish shame: start to tell our own truths.

The Time Is Now to Tell Our Stories

For the past two decades there's been an upswell in speech—celebrities, reality stars, and real people alike; on air, in interviews, online and in print, on social media and in real life—leading to a May 2023 essay in *Glamour* about what Hanna Lustig calls "the golden age of oversharing."

Lustig defines oversharing as the revelation of "stuff nobody really wants to know—the kind of thing that would make someone tweet, 'She could've kept that to herself,'" and traces the roots of this to Reddit and legacy Subreddits like r/confessions, shadowy spaces that preceded the female personal essay boom of the 2010s. Dubbed the "first-person industrial complex" in *Slate* by Laura Bennett, Bennett says "young people scrap[ed] their interior lives in order to convert the rawest bits into copy" for sites like *Gawker*, *BuzzFeed*, Medium, and of course, *xoJane*, a website known for what Jia Tolentino described in the *New Yorker* as a "certain kind of personal essay that, for a long time, everybody seemed to hate." Boundary-pushing personal dramas garnered zillions of clicks and comments, including reactionary articles and reviews barbed with personal, sneering attacks. "It does no favors to young female writers to convince them that they are courageous voices in the wilderness for dedicating their talents to writing stories that are received as lurid, not literary," the writer Hamilton Nolan wrote in a post about one such writer, Alt Lit sensation Marie Calloway, on *Gawker*. "Let's all shut up more in 2012."

Shut up we did not. Instead, we wrote candidly about pregnancy loss, childhood sexual assault, domestic violence, and the tampon we left in our vagina for weeks. Sure, some of us could've used an editor and/or therapist, but our work's impact was undeniable. By renegotiating the boundaries between the public and private sphere, we were breaking down an implicit collective enforcement that shame depends on. We were confronting a long, sexist history of being excluded from the public sphere, having realized it was to our individual and collective peril to keep these stories to ourselves.

All this confessional storytelling was a precursor to the #MeToo movement. The phrase was first used in 2006 by organizer Tarana Burke to support survivors of sexual assault. A decade later, the idea took off as a hashtag after actress Alyssa Milano wrote a tweet inviting women to share their experiences online publicly so they might "give people a sense of the magnitude of the problem."

"When #MeToo went viral on October 15, 2017," Tarana Burke recalled for *Time*, "millions of people around the world made a courageous decision to reveal their darkest secrets. The sheer number— 12 million responses on social media in 24 hours—ensured that the stories could not be ignored." In spite of critics intent on calling us tiresome, lacking talent, slutty, and definitely absolutely not at all interesting enough to even mention so really just stop talking already, no seriously, just shut up, we talked on, in print and online, until, as Hannah Lustig wrote, "our collective threshold for oversharing is much higher."

The golden age of oversharing, according to Lustig, is due at least in part to these personal-essay-penning pioneers. It's also on account of the pandemic, Lustig says, which further blurred the lines between the personal and professional when folks everywhere were compelled to work from home. The proliferation of social media, too, Lustig says, has made people more comfortable with being honest. Not only can people still post anonymously on any platform from a pseudonymous account, but you can post under your real name and receive support from your in-real-life friends.

There is still backlash; we don't let it stop us. The cost of silence is too great.

Waking Up from Denial

"From the ages of twelve to twenty-five, shame stole my ability to truly dream," writes Keah Brown in an essay published in the anthology *You Are Your Best Thing*, a must-read collection of Black writers reflecting on shame and vulnerability. "I cared only about surviving and let shame convince me that no one genuinely cared about me."

As a queer Black woman with cerebral palsy, Brown says her greatest desire was to be normal. Her website describes how "through years of introspection and reaching out to others in her community, she reclaimed herself and changed her perspective. Writing became a refuge from the steady stream of self-hate that strengthened inside her."

Then Brown's hashtag #disabledandcute went viral. "I was getting death threats for weeks," Brown later recalled for her audience on Twitter. "Every possible disability-related joke or insult was pushed in my direction. Like people were really telling me to kill myself over my desire to be seen."

Why does this happen? "Our society has no idea what to do with the genuine feelings and humanness of women," Brown explains in the essay. According to Brown, shame weaponized against women doesn't get to her: "I will feel, be, and do as much as I want proudly for the rest of my life. To be vulnerable and emotional as a Black woman is to live in power, which I take back every day, not apologizing for who I am or the space I take up as I move through the world.

"Talking about our experiences is how we move forward," Brown continues. "And honestly, I am tired of where we are. We deserve true, lasting change as a nation and the ability to exist in a world that sees people like me as full human beings."

Brown's words remind me of a quote by Susan Griffin from her book, *A Chorus of Stones*: "What is hidden, kept secret, cannot be loved. It exists in a place of exile."

For years after my mother's rejection, I lived in this place—a kind of loveless exile. There was no part of me that wished to be revealed, which is to say loved. I threw myself full force in the opposite direction. It was as if I had become the pain. Anger radiated off me. It felt almost erotic, powerful and hot. I felt protected by its force, but it was exhausting.

I called my mom every Sunday. I called her because I'd have felt guilty if I didn't. I called because if I didn't, I knew she wouldn't call me. When we talked, we skated over the past like a frozen pond. We stayed on neutral topics like the weather. She'd tell me the plot of the last movie she'd seen. I'd ask how she was doing and she'd say, "Fine." She didn't ask about me.

The truth, I suspected in the very deepest parts of me, was that not everything was fine. Still, I turned away from my unnamed feelings and told myself to be happy. I told myself I had no reason to feel sad.

Everything was fine. *So why do I always feel like something is wrong? Why am I always so irritable? Why do I feel so much pressure, all the time, to always be the best—the best at everything? Better than everyone else? Why do I feel like the worst? A bad daughter? A shitty girlfriend? A horrible sister? A terrible employee? A useless friend?*

There was, of course, some truth to this—I was not, and had not for some time, been living up to my ideals. There was a hell of a lot of space between—as Brené Brown would put it—my practiced values (what I did, thought, and felt) and my aspirational values (what I wanted to do, think, and feel). When our behavior is in conflict with our ideals, we feel ashamed, and because of shame we can't reflect honestly on our behavior or the behavior of others. Without insight, I couldn't hold myself or anyone to account.

In her essay "The Wisdom of the Process" in *You Are Your Best Thing,* Prentis Hemphill calls pain aversion "one of the central motivators in American culture" and describes the great lengths people go to in order "to win our way to a pain-free culture." Hiding, denying, and transferring shame is not only our individual way of life, Hemphill says, but a collective coping mechanism, and an explanation for oppression: we "shape the world to outsource suffering and create structures to concentrate this pain and mythologies of superiority to justify it."

But pain serves a purpose. "When experienced at a digestible rate, when our belonging and safety are not at risk, it can develop us," Hemphill says. "It can sturdy our sense of ourselves and open up the capacity for empathy. It can remind us that much of what there is to feel can be felt."

It is very difficult to acknowledge everything we have spent our entire lives denying, and that everyone around us insists we deny. Deran Young is a licensed clinical therapist and founder of Black Therapists Rock, an organization committed to improving the social and psychological well-being of vulnerable communities. In the essay "Honoring Our Stories, Transforming Our Pain" in *You Are Your Best Thing*, she likens her experience of acknowledging the impact of racism to "walking into a big, dark, murky cave." Young writes,

> You know that once you go in there, you're not going to be able to see, you're not going to know where you're going or what you'll find. But you walk in anyway because you know there are things in that cave that you need to reclaim, things that have been taken from you. You walk in despite the fear, to reclaim your ability to speak up and say what you need—to be seen and heard, and to take up space.

For so much of my life I felt irredeemable. I had so much, then, to reclaim. When I look back at the years I lost to shame, the years of feeling around blindly in the dark of my self-hatred, I recognize and honor the bravery this took.

"I have great compassion for the parts of me that didn't want to hope or dream because they carried a deep fear of disappointment," writes Young. "I had to admit that deep down inside, I had been carrying years of anger and despair."

Letting Go of Self-Blame

It's so familiar, so ubiquitous, that it's become our own inner monologue: if there isn't physical proof, it didn't happen. If there is evidence, you're setting the dude up. You didn't tell anyone, and so you must be lying. If you confided in friends, they're part of the hoax. If you didn't seek medical treatment, you weren't injured; if you did seek medical treatment, you overreacted. It was all part of a vindictive plan.

What were you wearing? What were your intentions? Were you

drinking or using drugs? Have you ever? Do you have a clear memory of the assault? Did you cut off contact with the abuser just as soon as it happened? Did you tell the perpetrator right then and there that what he did was wrong? Why not? Why didn't you speak up? Why didn't you say no? Why didn't you fight back? If you fought back, you were the aggressor.

No matter what you do, be prepared for it to be wrong. And prepare yourself for the world to feel sorry for the man who violated you.

Writer and philosopher Kate Manne is credited with coining the word "himpathy" to describe the outsized sympathy extended to male perpetrators of misogyny and sexual violence over their female victims, who are often erased in the process. As Manne puts it, "Himpathy means worrying about his bright future, not her suffering."

A perfect victim is a victim, entirely. She is—before, during, and after the event—completely without fault. That is to say she is without agency. A victim has no choices. But real women have choices. Before, after, and sometimes even in the midst of our most powerless moments, we have power. We make decisions. We make choices and, yeah, sometimes we make mistakes.

When I ask Abby if she was a victim, she pauses. Asks for some time to answer. Emails a week later. "Was I a victim of the parents who verbally abused me when I was a child? Yes. Was I a victim of the man who assaulted and robbed me at gunpoint? Absolutely. Was I a victim of the professor who enticed me, in the name of collegiality and friendship, with promises of publishing success, even as he groomed me as a sexual conquest (whom he later discarded and delegitimized)? I'm still not entirely sure."

It was consensual, she maintains, but it was an abuse of power: "He humiliated me."

Having an affair with her professor was a mistake.

"He was a very charming person," she recalls. "And I was charmed—and ambitious."

Abby was thirty-seven when she signed up for a continuing education class in creative writing at a local college, hoping to jumpstart a career in journalism.

"Like a lot of women in their thirties, I was at the point where it's like, okay, is shit gonna happen or not? You know, am I going to be someone who had promise in her youth and faded out, or someone who gets a chance to break out of the pack and do something?"

Her instructor was a fortysomething-year-old local journalist, tall, thin, and soft-spoken, a man Abby describes as "sexy ugly." ("You know when a guy is not handsome but they have a certain swagger that appeals to women? That was him.")

One day after class he called Abby aside and said, "You really have a knack for this, we should have lunch and talk about it."

They met at a local chicken place and talked shop. Abby was married at the time, so she didn't think much of it. "It was all about the work, and opportunities in journalism."

Soon after, the instructor introduced Abby to the editor of a local newspaper, and she became a regular contributor. He helped her place a piece at another, even more prestigious publication.

A few months after that first encounter, Abby says, "he would start saying things like, Oh, you drive me crazy, but I love it, you know, or—not quite that overt. More like, Are you trying to drive me crazy? You know, Are you trying to be difficult to give me a hard time? And there were, like, these winks and things and the little casual brushes. Then one day there was a hug. And then one day, there was, like, a longer hug, and then there was a kiss. And then it was, like, What are we doing? Oh my god, what are we doing? But by then all the groundwork had been laid."

After nights out with her instructor, Abby would come home to her husband in front of the TV, with his headphones on, surfing the Web, a cigar burning in the ashtray next to him. "It was safe to assume he'd been drinking, but he hid that from me. We went from companions to having no connection."

Abby says she felt no shame at the time. "If my husband had been the man he appeared to be on the surface, and here I was, trading sexual favors for access to my dream, I would have felt more shame." But because he was an alcoholic and their marriage was an unhappy one, Abby says, "I could justify it."

A year after it began, Abby says the instructor started edging her out. "Finding newer and younger, hotter women. Fresh meat."

One day Abby caught a glimpse of a text, where some other woman was talking about what a great kisser he was. "It wasn't like a cloud burst," Abby says, "but the rain started."

To this day, Abby wonders what might've happened had she not allowed this male mentor "access to me, and all the good, juicy bits of me. Would the gatekeeping have really been as locked down tight as I feared it would otherwise? Would I have found a way to break into work?"

What might've happened had Abby not, as she describes it, made a "dick move"?

Over email, Abby says, "I said something like, this isn't working—maybe it's time to come clean. It was so out of character—I don't threaten people—but I was just so mad."

He didn't respond. Instead, Abby says, "He started cutting all the ties, and spreading rumors and just at every level of every relationship that I had forged on my own with my own work. You know, he went out there and said stuff that was so demeaning and diminishing that people just started fleeing from even knowing me.

"The disconnect between what you know to be real and the reality this man was putting out there, I just couldn't reconcile it—and that's why I became determined to talk about it," Abby says.

Instead of giving up on her dream to become a writer, she committed herself even further to her art. Then, even though it threw her into financial crisis, Abby left her marriage. She went on to write and perform a comical essay about getting foreclosed on after the divorce "because nobody wants to hear about women facing homelessness. So I made it kind of funny and outrageous, and people were horrified and aghast, which is how I knew it was hitting the mark."

Looking back, she says the whole situation turned her into a crazy bitch—"We're talking major therapy and pharmacological intervention," she says with a laugh. But in the years since, Abby says, "There are so many women that I have encountered who were the crazy bitch, you know, for all different kinds of circumstances. It made me realize: maybe *crazy bitch* is not such a bad thing."

Bringing Truth into the Light

In her groundbreaking book *Trauma and Recovery*, psychologist Judith Lewis Herman spells out recovery as unfolding in three steps. The first step, she says, is establishing safety. From there, a survivor can begin putting back together their narrative and sharing their story, which is step two. The third step is reconnecting to others. For many, reconnection requires adapting some kind of "survivor mission"—a reason for being that makes sense of the pain.

"Remembering and telling the truth about terrible events are pre-requisites for the restoration of the social order and for the healing of individual victims," Herman writes. She adds, "The conflict between the will to deny horrible events and the will to proclaim them aloud is the central dialectic of psychological trauma."

One way or another, our greatest shame wills itself into the light; until it does, we remain sick as individuals and sick as a culture.

The first time I cheated on Rick happened in Mexico, some weeks before I'd started working at La Trampa. He was a local boy, sixteen years old, with curly brown hair and contacts that turned his brown eyes blue. I'd met him at the grocery store where he worked. Paco loved all things American—American clothes and American movies, he even preferred American food—and so I was devastated when he came to me, the day after the first time we slept together, and he told me it was over. He had a new girlfriend, he told me, "a Mexican girl."

He said it with such pride, it almost felt as if he was trying to hurt me.

Before this, Rick had been the only guy I'd ever slept with. Now, I thought, what we'd had was ruined. It'd been a mistake I vowed to never do again, but I broke that promise. Having done it once, it was as if I couldn't stop. I cheated on Rick three times in Mexico, with three different guys. After the fourth time it happened—the next semester, back on campus—I stopped counting. I told myself the cheating didn't count. What happened in the club was work. So what if I sometimes enjoyed it? I was allowed to enjoy my job. Shame would not allow me to acknowledge my wrongs. I could not own the part I played in my pain.

In the months and years that followed, I completed my London internship and spent some time back on campus before making my way to New York City for my fifth and final internship. By the time I arrived in the Big Apple, I'd been dancing in clubs on and off for three years. That semester I worked in development at a nonprofit after-school program for underprivileged girls. In my off-hours, I got a job at FlashDancers in Times Square.

At FlashDancers, surrounded by the most gorgeous, glamorous women I'd ever seen in real life, I was constantly trying to convince myself that I was beautiful enough to be working there. Sometimes I made myself beautiful by believing it so. *If only I believe it hard enough*, I told myself, *then others will also. Everyone*, I told myself, *is falling for my act.*

I called Rick, still living back in Cincinnati, nearly every day. Whatever I said to him, I still didn't tell him that I was stripping and I sure as hell didn't tell him that I was sleeping with Jay, some guy I'd met through my day job. Jay was an out-of-work musician who ran errands for my boss. He was exactly the kind of underachiever I gravitated toward—a man with flaws so glaringly obvious they deflected from my own shortcomings.

Why, Jay—a *grown-ass adult*—didn't even have an apartment of his own; he was staying on a friend's couch. My roommate didn't much like Jay or the fact he came over in the middle of the night—high on coke, locked out of his friend's place, ringing our bell with nowhere else to go. I let Jay in because I liked the company. I liked to smoke Jay's cigarettes and I liked that Jay needed me, if only for a place to crash.

Jay and I didn't use condoms. If you'd asked me then why I wasn't on birth control, I might've said that I didn't know where to get it. I might've told you the pill made me sick. I'd been on the pill, I might've explained, and when I missed one and doubled up the next day, it made me so nauseous I would sometimes throw up. I couldn't remember to take a pill each day, and I didn't like condoms. That's what I would have told you. But it was more than that. In my mind, I shouldn't have even been having sex. Lying and cheating was wrong—so wrong, there was no way to make it right. Using a condom, somehow, would be like acknowledging my betrayal.

My last month alone in New York City, I missed my period. The week that it was supposed to have come came and went and then another. Three weeks late, I took a pregnancy test in Jay's friend's bathroom. I sat on the toilet, staring at the cruddy powder blue tile, waiting the agonizing minute. When the test came back negative, I felt an enormous sense of relief.

Two weeks later, I still hadn't gotten my period. A second test came back positive.

When I told Jay I was pregnant he said something like if you decide to keep it, I'll be there for you and I'll support you and your decision. I laughed and said, "Jesus Christ, Jay, you can't even take care of yourself."

I was so angry, so determined to not be a child, to need no one, to hold myself together. My mother drove me in silence to the appointment and I paid for it myself.

In the clinic waiting room there was a scrapbook in which patients were invited to write down their feelings and thoughts. I remember wanting to write something—to say something, anything. Where so many women who'd come before me had written of grief, I had nothing to say. I wrote nothing. So adept at not feeling my feelings, I could not go back to access them now, even when I wanted to. In this moment, I could feel nothing.

The abortion became one more thing that Rick couldn't know about, another source of shame unseparated from the rest.

After Rick and I had both graduated from college and moved to New York City, I stopped stripping and got a "real" job working in development at the last nonprofit I'd interned for. I told myself to move on. I went about evading shame in all the ways we do: alcoholism, perfectionism, workaholism, issues with food and exercise—I did it all.

At night, I'd curl into him on the couch while we watched TV, willing myself to forget everything that had happened. I would tell myself I was lucky to have him. I would do nothing to jeopardize his love. Never mind all the ways we were incompatible; I depended on Rick for things I didn't allow myself to comprehend.

In the years since, I have written about the abortion. In at least two published essays, I have described the procedure as no big deal. In a piece for *xoJane*, I described what was removed from me as "a clump of cells." "I Don't Regret My Abortion—and Neither Do 98 Percent of Women," the title of one of my articles shamelessly proclaimed.

But the story changed years later, when I had my IUD removed and a doctor suggested I'd have trouble carrying a baby to term on account of scarring in my uterus, possibly from the abortion. I felt, in that moment, as if my medical condition were a punishment. I imagined my uterus with the complexion of Freddy Krueger. I was dirty, damaged, my scarred-up vagina evidence that I was too compromised to become a mom. I felt shame, and so I wrote about those feelings, too.

Phew, that was a hard essay to write. It was difficult, even after years of recovery, to admit that I empathized with the feelings of abortion regret commonly amplified by the anti-choice movement, just as it was hard years earlier to admit when anti-sex-work rhetoric touched on certain truths. Our feelings are complicated, and complicated even further by shame.

These days, whatever the feelings, I have places where and people with whom I can express them, and I know that doing so will help me make sense of them. Without these mirrors, I could not be honest and honestly reflect, and without reflection, we cannot change.

The Power of the Pen

Back then I had no one.

I did, however, have my journals.

Well before—and after—my story ended up in the callused, careless hands of Larry Fagin, spiral notebooks served as safe containers for my most untamed thoughts. Even without an audience, putting pen to paper was good for my mental and physical health.

"Writing saved my life," Michelle says. "It's the rehearsal space I use to prepare for tough conversations. It gives me the courage and poise I need to set boundaries. My journal is a trustworthy vault for all my secrets."

"Writing led to wisdom I never anticipated," Tamara says. "It led to empathy for people and situations I'd been destroying myself over for decades, knowledge of how to balance boundaries, and insight into not just who I really am but what my true purpose is in this life."

Jamie Schler reflects on her experience writing a personal essay for the *Washington Post* about her brother's illness: "It took me a long, long time writing before I pitched it," she says, but doing so "helped me confront the grief I felt from his death. Now I'm starting to write about my depression, panic, anxiety, and I hope it also helps me in the same way, facing it, thinking deeply about it from there . . . I don't know yet."

"As much as I want the story out there because I think it will help others," a different Jamie, Jamie Beth, admits, "the writing is healing to me because it's allowing me to give structure to the mess of memories and emotions I have swirling in my brain.

"Before I started piecing the book together," Jamie Beth continues, "thoughts in my head were very loud and often contradictory. Now that I see them on the page, my mind has quieted a bit, and I can see better how two seemingly opposite things can be true at once."

"The first draft is just you telling yourself the story," author and humorist Terry Pratchett once said. From here, and with a bit of emotional distance, you can begin to reflect on the meaning of the events.

This reflexive process of integrating experience with reflection is pivotal in the process of "narrative therapy," a therapeutic approach developed in the 1970s and '80s by New Zealander David Epston and his Australian colleague Michael White.

In narrative therapy, a patient is encouraged to conceptualize her past self as nonessentialized—to see herself in relation to her problems rather than defined by them. The same therapeutic process naturally happens when we write in memoir and personal essay. In those forms, the writer naturally appears in the story as two people: the protagonist—that is, the character inhabiting the action (who you were then)—and an older, wiser narrator (who you are now), the voice telling the reader what happened and reflecting on what it all meant.

Memoir-writing workshops were my first experience sharing with a "safe container" beyond a notebook and a pen. Twelve-step groups came next. This term, "safe container," was used by Judith Herman and refers to an environment where individuals or group members can feel safe to be themselves and tell the truth. Both writing groups and twelve-step programs are organized around the candid disclosure and sometimes critical examination of its participants' experiences. Even when shared without comment, personal stories told in the first person illuminate for the teller the meaning of the transpired events. Telling a potentially shameful story to a group is better than sharing it with an individual, Herman says, because a group is stable enough to hold or "contain" what may feel too intimate to share with any one person.

The truth is never as terrible, or titillating, as shame makes it out to be. By writing and sharing my stories, I felt, for the first time ever, a certain freedom from a fear-driven mind. Shadowy sensations that had terrified me stepped out into the light and shrunk down to size. Eventually, I began to integrate these feelings, and their origin stories, back into the fabric of my everyday life.

Finding the Right Audience

Disclosure, and writing in particular, is a powerful therapeutic tool. At the same time, becoming vulnerable makes us—well, vulnerable.

Just as soon as it happened, and for years after, I convinced myself that Larry Fagin's indecent proposal hadn't affected me. And yet, within a year of our meeting, I quit my day job, just as Larry Fagin suggested. This action set off a chain of unfortunate, distressing, and—yes—shameful events. I ignored his suggestion that I not pursue an MFA and enrolled at the New School, but I held on to a lot of the deep-seated beliefs about what it meant to be a writer that my meeting with Larry had confirmed. These beliefs extended beyond my writing. They affected my sense of self-worth and my place in the world.

Let's talk about the people in our lives who reinforced our shame. Maybe some of these people are still in our lives. People who'll let you believe you're the biggest piece of shit on the planet because you spent your daycare money on designer jeans to impress a blind date and now you're broke. Okay, we're human. We do dumb shit. We make mistakes.

Do the people in your life seize an opportunity to make you feel small, magnify your flaws, and reinforce your negative self-talk?

Consider the following examples:

My ex and his girlfriend sent me a long text about not making sure all my daughter's homework was completed. My face flushed and my stomach dropped. I felt instantly sick. I responded defensively, which was probably not the best response but those two really gang up and bulldoze me. I never know how to stand up for myself.

One of my coworkers has been on this job location for over twenty years. Never mind the fact that it was her job to train us, she makes me and other colleagues feel bad because we don't know the job as well as she does.

I slept with someone who, turns out, was a real jerk. He tried to shame me for it in front of our mutual friends and make me seem like a slut. It felt mortifying.

No matter our crime, we deserve compassion. We deserve people in our lives that honor our capacity for change and don't exploit our vulnerabilities. Ever since her first child was born, Jenn has recognized that childhood trauma has been triggered, leading to sometimes explosive rage.

"My toddler still wakes up a few times a night, and sometimes he's inconsolable and cries a lot, which is triggering for me because I wasn't allowed to cry as a kid," Jenn says.

"One night I was so enraged that I yelled at him, 'Why don't you go to fucking sleep?!' I yelled so loud that it woke my husband up."

Instead of criticizing his wife and reinforcing her shame, Jenn says, her husband offered to switch with her and take over the job of monitoring their son's sleep for the night.

"I felt relieved," Jenn says, "but also ashamed. I accepted his offer of help, but I felt incompetent, and not good enough as a mother."

They talked about the incident in couple's therapy, Jenn says, and both the therapist and her husband undermined shame's message of secrecy at all costs by offering compassion and understanding.

"I'm learning that when I'm dysregulated, it's okay to ask for help," Jenn says, "and that needing help doesn't make me a bad mother. On the contrary, when I struggle as a mother, the more I ask for help, the better I can be."

It's already been said that you can't shame yourself into positive change. You can't bully yourself or someone you love into giving up an addiction, losing weight, or leaving an unhealthy relationship. I know what happens when I'm hard on myself: I feel frustrated and powerless. I get mad and then sad. And then mad again. I get defensive. And so it goes, until I give up. Studies testify I'm not unique. For example, authors behind a 2019 article published in the *Canadian Medical Association Journal* found that fat shaming "is linked to depression, anxiety, low self-esteem, eating disorders, and exercise avoidance," and testify that the more people are exposed to weight bias and discrimination, "the more likely they are to gain weight and become obese, even if they were thin to begin with. Researchers say they're also more likely to die from any cause, regardless of their body mass index."

These days, the moment I recognize that I'm feeling ashamed—when I'm not acting in alignment with my ideals or am more invested in other people's approval than myself and my goals, I can usually recalibrate very quickly. I acknowledge the tightness in my stomach. I stop fighting and soften. I forgive myself for whatever damage I've done.

It's not always easy, but I try to show others the same compassion. Whatever the trespass, I don't believe in shaming individuals for bad behavior—that includes shaming people for committing sexual assault or for having a poor consent practice. Shame, as I've just said, doesn't work. There are better, more effective alternatives to ostracization and criminalization. I love this truth spoken by author, activist, and spoken-word poet Sonya Renee Taylor in an interview with *Ensemble* magazine on the topic of transformative justice: "The ability to figure out how to live amongst, forgive and still in many cases, love and marry and procreate with people who have caused you great, great harm is actually something marginalized communities around the world [have] figured out how to do every single day."

It is possible to address unacceptable actions and harmful behavior in a way that's gentler on all of us. In a 2021 TEDx Auckland Talk: "Let's Replace Cancel Culture with Accountability," Taylor observes that challenging oppression by calling someone out activates the same parts of the brain that are triggered when you're on the receiving end: the threat response is activated and we feel in danger.

Calling someone out feels very personal—and dangerous—because it is: "As a woman of color, as a person who lives at the intersection of multiple marginalized identities, challenging oppression is an inherently threatening activity," Taylor says.

The social justice activist and educator talks about calling people *in* as one alternative to shaming them. Calling in means walking them through what happened, gently and generously letting them know exactly what they've done wrong, and suggesting what actions they can take to make it better. Calling in is a lot of work, "and puts an undue burden on the person harmed." Because calling someone in demands a lot of work, and because it, too, can trigger an amygdala response, Taylor presents a third option: call on a person to do the work by themselves. "I don't have to publicly berate you nor do I have to nuzzle you to my bosom and carry you gently to enlightenment. I can share with you how you harmed me and what you did, and entrust you with the work needed to repair that harm."

We've all been on both sides of this. We've all been guilty of harming someone, and we've all felt harm. We've all felt shame and acted out as a result.

When it comes to shame we are never "recovered" or "resistant." Shame resilience, as we will discuss in the next chapter, is a daily practice. Recovery from trauma means unlearning the unhealthy parts of our identity, letting go of habits we falsely believe are key to our survival. It means embracing vulnerability and confronting our fears, including the terror of scarcity and fear of looking uncool. Sometimes it means divesting from individuals and networks that harm us or lead us to behave in ways out of alignment with our beliefs.

I think of recovery and shame resilience as synonymous. Both are a struggle to trust people in a world where people have proven themselves untrustworthy. It's a struggle to accept those times when we have let ourselves down. It is a fight to feel safety in a world that is unsafe, to let go of control in a world that is terrifyingly uncontrollable, and to feel power, especially in circumstances when we fear we have none. Recovery is a process of becoming accountable to people, as well as holding people to account. It happens in real time and in real space—the space we occupy with our bodies. For years, I fought to take up space with my body. I did not honor it as a practice then, but long-distance running, yoga, and meditation were attempts to reacquaint myself with my body. I am learning to return to the body that had been more than confiscated from me, that had—as French writer and playwright Hélène Cixious says—been turned into an "uncanny stranger on display." I am on a journey to own my own breath. I am claiming every part of myself and my story, and that means leaving nothing out. What has happened cannot be undone, but it can be dealt with. I am not, and will never be perfect. It is still, to my shame, my habit to leave my body when someone does something to me that I don't like. Even now, in an effort to evade shame, I sometimes hurt myself. I sometimes hurt others. But I am dedicated to doing better—and I am on your side, so long as you are, too.

Not So Different After All

"Recognizing the invisible parts of oneself in another person can feel like a radiant kind of love," author Melissa Febos writes. "It can make those parts stronger inside you."

This is what happened when Brie, a friend from college, reentered my life. Some months after my run-in with Fagin, Brie came to town for a semester. After dating for nearly five years, Rick and I were heading toward marriage, even as the distance between us grew. Somehow I'd been able to keep the fact that I'd been stripping all those years a secret, and I continued to keep it a secret, even though we now lived under the same roof.

But with Brie there were no secrets. Brie and I could speak to each other the way I could speak in my journals, just whatever came out was alright.

My relationship with Brie was driven by my desire for newness, but it was more than just that. Brie and I were friends first. I trusted her. She cared about me. None of this changed when we started having sex.

Love enlivens, it frightens. It forces us to be vulnerable. I lost myself in the heat of its expression. When Brie and I first became lovers, the anxious feelings went away. I stopped obsessing over work. I still did a good job, I just didn't overthink it. My obsessive-compulsive rituals around diet and exercise relaxed. I got a taste of what my life was missing—which was intimacy. I loved Rick, but without honesty between us, our capacity to love each other was very small.

I reasoned with myself that the fact I was having an affair with a woman might be an explanation for everything. *This means I'm not normal*, I thought. *I'm different.* I told myself that if I told Rick this secret, he would know everything about me that he needed to.

One night, I told him: "I'm in love with her."

"Are you saying you want to break up?" There was a helpless and desperate tenor in his voice. He was near tears. I had never seen him cry.

"I don't know," I answered. *Coward.* I began to cry.

Later that week, Brie and I were having dinner together. I came home and the apartment was empty. Rick had gone out. The room was dark, so I turned on the light. I thought at first that we'd been robbed. All my journals, which had been tucked safely away in a trunk that had doubled as a coffee table, carpeted the hardwood floor. I thought we'd been ransacked. Then I noticed the books all lay open to particular pages.

Someone—it had not hit me yet who—had gone through my personal belongings and they'd found my journals and they'd read them. Somehow, they'd read everything. There it all was, all my horridness, all spelled out in my careful script. The betrayals. The secrets. My shame.

Whatever I'd intended when I'd told him about the affair—well, it didn't matter now. I'd assumed that if Rick ever found out all the secrets I'd kept from him, he'd have no choice but to leave me. Slowly, over the next week or so, it became apparent that he didn't want us to break up. The fact that he was willing to forgive me made me feel as if I had no choice but to stay. More time went by and we got engaged. Deep down, he was still angry, we were both confused, and I was ashamed. Eventually, I called the engagement off.

6

First Comes (Self) Love

Putting Ourselves First

"My barn having burned down," writes seventeenth-century Japanese poet Mizuta Masahide, "I can now see the moon."

I see the wisdom of this quote now, but when I left Rick, I could see nothing but darkness, not even the moon. Not that night, and not for a long time. I was a charred shell, nothing inside my body but worthlessness.

I drank to fill myself up. I drank to drown the darkness. I fucked anyone to feel something and still, I felt nothing. I felt nothing. I felt nothing. I felt nothing. Then I felt pain.

Some months after I left Rick, I started seeing a therapist. He referred me to a psychiatrist, who prescribed a bunch of pills that only made me feel more out of control. He also suggested I had an alcohol problem and recommended I try a twelve-step program. I most definitely did not take this suggestion—not at first. Instead, I started trading sex for cash. I would not have told you then, nor for some time, that I felt grief. Years later, with a journalist from *Marie Claire*, I would deflect my shame with a joke that maybe I was after The Boyfriend Experience. After I left Rick, I was lonely and, yes, I wanted the feeling of having a boyfriend without any of the responsibility.

And so I placed ads in the erotic services section on Craigslist. I advertised myself as a non pro—not a professional, just a college girl, bored and curious—and for the most part that is what I was.

I told myself that sex work was work, a job like any other—so what if I enjoyed it? The truth is that I didn't enjoy it so much as it offered a feeling of relief. When I wasn't working, I felt fragile, stressed out, and depressed. I never felt nourished, protected, or provided for. Not feeling particularly respected in any capacity, I fell further into despair.

For women who struggle with hypersexuality, our intimate relationships are compromised by intense feelings of need and fear. We question intimate relationships constantly and mistrust and withdraw from people while simultaneously seeking them out desperately. Shame is thought to be intrinsic in hypersexual behaviors, especially in women. I'm not talking about super sex-positive women having a lot of fun sex. I am talking about a repeat pattern of sexual encounters that left me feeling powerless, guilty, and disgusted with myself.

I sold sex online for approximately three months. No one forced me to do it or profited off my labor. It was my choice to start and it was my choice to stop. A month or so before I got sober, I migrated from the "erotic services" section to "Craigslist Personals" in search of a legitimate relationship. And yet, and try as I might, I couldn't stop myself from having quick, unsatisfying casual sex night after night. One night stands felt even more degrading than sex work; at least, as a prostitute, I had gotten paid.

Trading sex for cash was my choice. And yet I can see now how the choices I've made in my life, and at this time in my life in particular, are related to my earlier trauma: evidence of a characteristic propensity to reexpose myself, as if this time I might master new versions of my earlier pain. Substance abuse, compulsivity, promiscuity, sex work, excessiveness in all respects, recklessness in every way imaginable—looking back, I feel a tremendous amount of compassion for my past self and all that she lived through. I no longer feel ashamed. I feel grateful she found help.

When I finally dragged myself into my first twelve-step meeting, almost a year after my therapist suggested it, this was my moment of grace. From that night on, I stopped drinking and I stopped trading sex for cash. I can't explain why it worked. There are many legitimate criticisms of twelve-step programs, and I concede that it's a far from perfect model. It doesn't work for everyone, but it worked for me. So when I refer to "recovery" from shame, a lot of my language (as you'll see here) is couched in the language of twelve-step programs. Take from it what you wish and leave the rest.

For example: "Hitting rock bottom" is a phrase used to describe the tipping point at which an individual decides to change his or her behavior. In the context of addiction, it means reaching a point where we are spiritually, financially, physically, and emotionally at our lowest point. When it comes to shame, there may be a culmination of negative events that makes life as you know it unmanageable. You might feel as hopeless as I did—but you don't need to. You don't need to hit rock bottom to initiate enduring, positive change in your life. You can start today. Reading this book and looking critically at the role shame plays in your life, that's a first step.

For Elle, there wasn't one big aha moment when her shame coalesced into behavior change. "There were, like, little turning points," Elle says of the end of her marriage. "A bunch of money had been stolen—taken out of our joint account—without any explanation as to why that had happened. There was a time when a line was crossed about, like, some physical violence. To me, there couldn't be a coming back from that." But it was still hard to cut through the denial and admit that something was wrong. "When things look so good from the outside. It was so hard to face the shame and admit the truth and say I was spit on in my home, where I live with my children," she says.

"I remember reaching out to some people. And I was like, 'I'm really scared for my safety. I'm sleeping in my room with the door locked by myself.' And people were like, 'Oh, he would never.' And I'm like, Oh my god, this is how people die. Because they say, 'I'm scared' and people don't listen to them."

Another turning point, Elle recalls: "I sent out a Christmas card. Everybody matched. It was a perfect picture. What a lie. I looked back at that picture and decided I would never send another Christmas card after that."

Elle initiated divorce. In the midst of their separation, she had a relapse of an eating disorder that she had struggled with for many years. "It became very real and scary," she admits about that time in her life. But once again, Elle struggled to reconcile outside appearances with what was happening on the inside "because everyone's like, 'Oh, you look so great!' And really I wanted to be like, 'I am so struggling right now!' But that's not an easy conversation to have with someone when they're just, like, casually commenting on your appearance.

"But actually," Elle says, "that is what it took to recover: I became entirely open about it, all of the time. I just put it out there, again and again. I just got to a point in my life where I'm like—well, I had dealt with some bullshit for so long, I wasn't gonna do that anymore.

I weeded out people really quickly until I homed in on those I could trust."

Elle couldn't afford inpatient therapy as she healed from her eating disorder so she did everything on an outpatient basis. She worked with a counselor and a dietitian. She also went to AA meetings to listen and better understand her ex-husband's experience, as well as Al-Anon, a twelve-step program specifically for relatives and friends of alcoholics.

Running has played a big role in her recovery, Elle says. For individuals recovering from disordered eating, "there's a fine line between doing it in a healthy and unhealthy way," so Elle worked with a specialist in sports medicine.

Elle says she learned to build in rest, focused on her breath, "and really started to listen to my body."

"In the beginning," Elle continues, "I would go into the woods, and I would just scream and scream. And it was fueled by so much pain that just drove me out there. I would just cry in the woods. It was the place I could just really get everything out. And there was no one judging me there. And, you know, as I healed and moved through that more and more, that pain was just slowly replaced by joy. And I never thought the pain would be replaced by joy, but it was."

Let Down Your Shield

Let's talk for a moment about the suffering of self-criticism. First off, let's not beat ourselves up over beating ourselves up. After all, as psychologist, author, and meditation teacher Tara Brach says, "We're fault-finding beings."

One of the core domains of spiritual awakening is stopping the war against ourselves, Brach says, and not reacting to our imperfections. "Freedom comes from the acceptance of the life right here, an unconditional caring presence with our life just as it is."

Radical acceptance, as Brach calls it, is the capacity to pause and be fully present with what is, and who we are, in this exact moment. Brach and other spiritual teachers point out that it's the nature of nature to have imbalance, asymmetry, and faults. Imperfection is intrinsic to all life-forms. We are all subject to conditioning and forces outside our control.

When we take our imperfect leanings personally and think we're uniquely defective, we are disconnected from our nature, our truth. A fear of making mistakes and admitting our imperfections—that is, our vulnerability—keeps us from knowing ourselves or being known. As Brené Brown writes in *Daring Greatly*, "Our willingness to own and engage with our vulnerability determines the depth of our courage and the clarity of our purpose; the level to which we protect ourselves from being vulnerable is a measure of our fear and disconnection." When we wait for perfectionism and invulnerability, Brown says, "we ultimately sacrifice relationships and opportunities that may not be recoverable, we squander our precious time, and we turn our backs on our gifts, those unique contributions that only we can make."

In *The Gifts of Imperfection* Brown talks about how letting go of perfectionism, and the fear of what people think, cultivates authenticity. We become more creative and joyful. We let go of our need for certainty and we lean into intuition and trust. We stop trying to look cool and in control and let ourselves laugh, sing, and dance.

Shame resilience isn't easy. For a lot of us, it means learning to compensate for the failures of adult protection and care. It means relearning how to live, mid-life.

It isn't easy, but it's possible. No matter what you've lived through or what age or point in your life, it is possible to recover your sense of self-worth. And actually, life becomes a lot more fun. Shame resilience can turn a will to die, an impulse to destroy, and a desire for destruction into the willingness to try, to hope, to create. To love. With all our severe impairments, people who've experienced traumatic life experiences have extraordinary strengths and remarkable creative gifts.

Somehow, by the grace of who-the-fuck-knows-what, I came to realize my own remarkable gifts. I reconstructed my story and with it I constructed a positive value of self, a meaningful order of creation. I reclaimed my place in the world. In recovery, I was offered an opportunity to live by a new set of principles. Sobriety, I was taught, meant that I would have to learn to pass up instant gratification in exchange for the dreams and ambitions I had tossed aside. It was an opportunity to become just one person versus two—the unlovable person I feared I was on the inside and the "I don't give a fuck" person I presented to others. Both these versions of me were false. In recovery, they said, I could become the woman I was meant to be—and I did.

One Day at a Time

My first day of teaching coincided with my ninetieth day of sobriety. I showed up early in a pencil skirt and button-up shirt, my hair pulled into a bun. On the outside, I was the picture of how I thought a teacher ought to look. Inside, I was a trembling mess.

P.S. 70 served more than 1,600 children, mostly Hispanic and African American, in grades K–5, and was one of the most populated elementary schools in New York City. I was there by way of the New York City Teaching Fellows, a prestigious fellowship that took people from nontraditional careers and put them in struggling schools. Charged with teaching art and creative writing to kids across all grades, I would meet each of my twenty-eight classes once a week for forty-five minutes each class—over seven hundred students in total. Most students were labeled "limited in English proficiency," meaning they came from homes where English wasn't spoken. Many struggled academically. Ninety percent of all our students qualified for free lunch.

That first morning, I read a picture book meant for toddlers to a class of fifth graders. I spent an entire class period trying to get a group of kindergarteners to sit peacefully on the rug while I figured out their names, only to learn when the teacher returned that none of them spoke English.

Teaching was exhausting and I was terrible at it at first, but I was determined.

The following week, I walked into that same classroom of fifth graders and took a new approach. After everyone had settled, I handed out index cards. The room looked up at me expectantly. "Tell me the one thing you need me to know about you," I said.

There was a girl in that class that I would come to know well. Nadisha was twice the size of most kids her age and three times as big as her classmates because she'd been held back. She was behind academically, and easily frustrated. When frustrated, she'd create disruptions and distract the rest of the class. Kids like this made the whole room feel unsafe. Physical fights, in this classroom especially, were not uncommon.

Nadisha was tough, but if you looked closer, you saw the face of a child—and I never forgot what she shared on her index card on the first day that we met: "I need you to know my father died and I miss him."

My job, as I saw it, was to give my students permission to tell these kinds of truths and make art that represented their experiences. Together, my students and I explored new and familiar materials. We took risks and made discoveries. We made mistakes and we fixed them. Kids are quick to crumple up a piece of paper and take a new one but in Ms. Petro's art class there was no starting over, only turning whatever we'd begun into something else.

As far as the curriculum, I encouraged my students to write and draw what they saw in the world, just as I do now with adults: self-portraits accompanied by personal biographies, cityscapes with stories verbally describing their environments. Growing up in a world of secrets, my own childhood journals had been my place to break the silence and exorcise my need to confess. My childhood writing cataloged my every disturbing experience. On the page, I could admit things I didn't dare say out loud. So could they.

It wasn't easy, but I learned. We all did. Then, at the start of my third year as a teacher, the *New York Post* burned it all down.

It's Not Personal (No, *Really*)

A wildfire is the perfect metaphor. The internet shaming was fast, intense, and seemingly unending, summed up in a spate of inflammatory newspaper headlines: "Bronx Art Teacher Blabs About Exploits as Stripper, Hooker at Open Mic Event," "Prostitute Teacher a Reason to End Tenure, Says NYC Mayor," and "Media Hot for 'Prostitute Teacher.'"

In another *New York Post* headline, I was called an "idiot prosti-teacher." A photo caption in that same article read, "Attention whore." More offensive than my past, it seemed, was the fact I'd had the gall to talk about it. The women's lifestyle website that I would later write for, *The Frisky*, supposed it was "all part of Petro's media-savvy plan to get publicity for her upcoming memoir," which the writer called "disgusting." The *New York Daily News*, *Inside Edition*, and *Us Weekly* all sent their female reporters, women ironically similar to me—young professional writers themselves—to get in my face, demanding to know how I could refer to myself as a feminist. When I'd approach neighbors who'd been formerly friendly, they'd cross the street.

I held my head up high, but I was also human. I was angry and confused. I felt an extreme amount of cognitive dissonance. I was right, and I knew it. *I was right!* I believed.

But then: *How could the whole world be so wrong?*

Part of me hoped some good would come of it all—that people might actually read and absorb what I was trying to say in the *Huffington Post* essay that had started it all.

A bigger part of me feared that wouldn't happen. There was nothing positive about what was happening to me, I reminded myself constantly, mercilessly. People found me disgusting. They thought I was stupid. People that I knew from high school were laughing at me. They'd send friend requests because they'd heard what happened, and they were making fun of me. For years, I would get dick pics from men, along with messages telling me that they had fucked me. Asking for my current rate. For a very long time, in my mind, I became exactly what the *New York Post* said I was: a disgrace.

I have carried the shame of that experience for a decade. But ultimately, in the end, some good did come of it. Thanks to what happened to me, and—importantly—the way I dealt with it, there's not a shame story I can't relate to. I might not have had the exact details happen to me, but I know: the feeling is the same. Whether you're being called a prosti-teacher on the cover of a major newspaper or calling yourself a bad mom in your head after burning your kid's waffle, we all know shame.

Jackie tells me about her greatest shame: "My ex-husband could only get off by watching someone else be with me. I gave in to this indulgence only a few times."

The first time, Jackie says, "I cried. I felt used. I shut down. I felt degraded and not even like a human with her own mind and soul. To think of what I did, just to appease his appetite. Thinking I was making him happy at the cost of my own."

Jackie and her ex divorced in 2006: "I found out he told his family that I had openly just cheated on him with these people. He played the victim. I was crushed."

When in shame, Jackie says, "There's a sinking feeling in your stomach, the feeling of dread, a deep sadness, worthlessness, embarrassment and nausea all at once."

Fortunately, Jackie surrounded herself with women who knew, and reinforced, her truth.

"He never knew I confided in close friends." It was only a handful of people, she tells me, but that was enough. "They never judged. They reminded me that I didn't want to do any of that, but he wouldn't quit pleading and asking over and over and over and over.

"They helped me realize that I wasn't really a willing participant. They reminded me that I felt terrible, and disgusted. Yes, I consented. But I was coerced." Her ex continued to harass and slander her for years, she says, but "no matter what I heard or what he may have told anyone, it didn't matter. The harder he tried to shame me, the more secure in myself I became. Until I honestly didn't care."

Shame resilience is a reversal of the ways we've been indoctrinated to feel about ourselves. It means de-individualizing and normalizing the parts of ourselves and our experiences we've been taught to hide or deny. By admitting our truths and acknowledging vulnerabilities in what Brené Brown calls "mutually empathetic relationships"—a fancy term for friendships—we learn that much of what we feel ashamed of is senseless and arbitrary. And then, by developing critical awareness, we also learn that shame is in service of a world that tells us some bodies are more valuable than others by shaming those that deviate from the norm.

American philosopher and psychologist John Dewey defines reflective thinking as "an active, persistent, and careful consideration of a belief or supposed form of knowledge in light of the grounds that support it, and the further conclusions to which it tends to lead." It means taking an evaluative look at all those images and stories we are constantly being bombarded with that tell us in one way or another that we aren't good enough as is.

When you encounter a story that makes you question your self-worth, or the worth of another human, here are some questions you might ask:

Is this story factual?

How else could these facts be interpreted?

What details are being left out?

Who benefits from this narrative?

A lot of times, the intention behind the story is to manipulate its audience into feeling bad about themselves so that they buy something. Other stories serve to protect the powerful and reinforce the status quo.

The more critical awareness you develop, the more you can recognize unkindness when you see it. You see our culture of shame for what it is. This is not a world that defends the innocent. As a society, we do not value bodies we deem different. This world wants those parts of us dead—and no, we cannot simply ignore its call for us to end ourselves. Instead, we have to recognize its impact. And then we need to fight back.

"Speaking publicly helped me overcome a lot of shame. I feel like my place in this world as an adult survivor is to help other people. Because I've healed so much," Kelly says, "I have that ability, and a lot of survivors don't."

Over the years, I have amassed a beautiful collection of female friends—and thanks to this project, I had the opportunity to get to know many of them better. They included a handful of exceptional shame-resilient women like Kelly Wallace, who shared harrowing stories and told me the steps she took to transform her life.

"I was an incest survivor," Kelly begins. "My paternal grandfather molested me. There was a big legal cover-up on the part of my dad because the molestation and sexual abuse took place in the same county where my dad was working as an assistant district attorney.

"Because of all that," Kelly explains, "my early childhood was marked with a sense of, like, What is wrong with me? Why was I basically rejected by my family who said I was lying—that I had made up the story. There was also the legal system saying, We don't believe you. Because he was found not guilty."

At that time, Kelly says, she didn't understand that there was a prosecution rate of only 1.5 to 3 percent. "I didn't learn that until later in life," she says.

Without that critical awareness, "I felt like I should just apologize for my existence," Kelly says.

"It didn't just come overnight," Kelly says of her recovery. "I worked hard to be where I am today. I worked through it in therapy. I've done a lot of meditation work, and body scanning, too. I also worked on a memoir about what happened to me. And I launched a podcast."

Even though the details of their suffering differed, the steps women I spoke to took to recover from intense shameful experiences were similar. Nearly every individual I spoke to that I'd describe as shame resilient had engaged, at some point, in individual therapy. Most had done group therapy, too (including twelve step and Self-Management and Recovery Training, or SMART, a peer recovery group that is widely considered an alternative to twelve-step). Some were a part of a religious or spiritual community. Many had a meditation practice. They considered themselves writers or had another creative outlet, such as music or visual arts. Movement—including exercise and dance—connected them back to their bodies. A lot of women I talked to mentioned psychedelic therapy, too.

And friendships. Everyone talked about their friends, generously sharing their lives with others who share their lives just as generously with them—this is an antidote to shame. We all need people who reaffirm our inherent worth and value and validate our experiences. These relationships keep us alive. I don't just mean breathing, but thriving. Mutually empathetic relationships keep us living as our truest selves.

"I do a lot of trying to just really be where I am," Cat says of her mindfulness practice. "I try to see my thoughts as clouds. And really see the distinctions between them and me. I remind myself constantly that I'm not my faults. I am not my fears. I am not my shame.

"My shame is a visitor," Cat continues. "It may be a frequent visitor, but it's not me. It's here to tell me something, and the message might not be right, but I can give it its own space to make its voice heard, and then thank it. And then take back over and go on about my day. I realize it's often a part of my childhood that's still harmed, trying to tell me something. Trying to be heard this time. Like, 'I hear you. Thank you. I've got it now.' And then I move on."

Laura talked about the role of music in her treatment for Crohn's disease. "I wrote all of these intense songs during that journey. All the feelings, I sang them out. And on the other side, the need to tell my own story again and again went away. I didn't need to write about my own trauma anymore. The pain—the anger, sadness, grief, and self-loathing—was gone."

When I asked Shy where her resilience comes from, she talked to me about dance: "I loved to perform when I was younger, and so I started dancing again as an adult—this time for myself. As a survivor of sexual molestation and physical violence, I'm working on allowing myself to get lost in my movements and to not seek out approval of others or worry about their judgment."

So much starts by acknowledging our feelings rather than turning away from them.

"The word 'triggered' gets a lot of hate," writer Alyson Shelton reflects. "But it is such a great word. And it helps me understand what is happening when I'm having an emotional flashback. It helps me put it in a place where I can say, 'This is happening.' And I can wait until I'm in a safe place alone, or with a professional, to process it.

"I didn't take emotional flashbacks very seriously for a long time. I would just chastise myself. Like, why am I still feeling this way? Why can't I get over this? Why does it still affect me? The only way to reclaim myself is to acknowledge how much it does affect me, and that getting over it isn't the goal. Getting whole is the goal."

Getting Whole Is the Goal

I would not say I was shame resilient when the *New York Post* humiliated me on its cover, but I had been moving in that direction. In addition to individual therapy and a handful of twelve-step programs, I'd introduced meditation into my mix by way of a secular Buddhist community known as the Dharma Punx NYC.

Two or three times a week I'd journey by train from the Upper East Side to Williamsburg in Brooklyn, or lug my bike up the impossibly steep stairwell at their Manhattan location, to attend in-person gatherings. I dabbled in other Buddhist communities but felt more comfortable at this one, led by the guy covered head to toe in tattoos who talked openly about his own twelve-step journey.

Dharma Punx NYC offered a very practical, applicable, and accessible approach to the teachings of Buddha. There would be a brief talk followed by a guided meditation. I learned about the mettā, or loving-kindness, meditation, which involves mentally sending yourself and others goodwill, kindness, and warmth by silently repeating a series of mantras.

A loving-kindness practice interrupts the shame spiral and negative self-talk, and it puts us in the presence of our goodness and gladness, a place where nothing is missing and nothing is wrong. There is no "if only": *If only I were different. If only I had done something else. If only I'd been someone else.* Instead, it cultivates a feeling of "enough." *I am enough. I have enough. This moment is enough.* Loving-kindness helps us say yes to the present moment and respond to the next one with intelligence.

I recently discovered an even simpler practice called RAIN, an acronym coined by meditation teacher Michele McDonald and further developed by Tara Brach. RAIN is a tool for practicing mindfulness and compassion that uses the following four steps:

Recognize what is happening;
Allow the experience to be there, just as it is;
Investigate with interest and care;
Nurture with self-compassion.

According to Brach, what RAIN does—when we offer ourselves attention and we bring in that nurturing—is a kind of spiritual reparenting. We're bringing the presence and kindness we need to heal. RAIN rewires the brain, creating new neural pathways to feeling empowered, creative, loving, and lucid. It is a beautiful practice when difficult feelings arise, including shame or other feelings of inadequacy.

I took home what I learned and started each morning on the meditation mat. Then I'd empty whatever was left in my head into a journal. A couple of friends and I had a gratitude practice. We'd each write a list of things we were grateful for and, throughout the day, exchange our lists over email. Their emails served as constant reminders that kept gratitude at the forefront of one's mind.

These programs and practices were helping reacquaint me with the feelings I thought I had to disavow. It introduced me to the truth that even "negative" feelings have texture and nuance.

The term "emotional granularity" describes the ability to differentiate between our emotions with specificity. I first talked about emotional granularity in a 2019 essay for the health and wellness publication *Elemental* by Medium. In that essay I talk about the work of Lisa Feldman Barrett, neuroscientist and author of the book *How Emotions Are Made: The Secret Life of the Brain*, who argues that emotions are not built into our brains at birth. Instead, Barrett says, our brains construct emotions in the moment by linking physical sensations to past experiences.

Our nervous system reacts similarly to negative emotions such as anger, fear, or frustration. Your pulse quickens, the breath shallows, your face flushes, and your muscles tense. Someone with low emotional granularity might clump these feelings together and label them more broadly: "I feel bad." Whereas someone with high emotional granularity can differentiate one "bad" feeling from another: sadness versus disappointment, anger versus indignation, impatience versus despair. The brain mitigates the danger by releasing certain amounts of cortisol and adrenaline depending on how it interprets the situation. The more granular the emotional palette, Barrett says, the more appropriate and efficient your nervous system will be at containing and managing a bad mood.

Emotional granularity doesn't just help us accurately label our own feelings; it also helps us infer the emotions of others. For instance, let's say you suggest to your husband you hire a babysitter because you could use a date night together. You will respond differently to your husband when you check your gut reaction and accept a frown to mean he's thinking deeply about how to make that happen rather than that he'd rather stay home.

Remember when Annie's husband called her out for eating four ice cream sandwiches in one sitting? Annie tells me the insensitive comment led to a multiday conversation about food choices. It was *insensitive*, Annie says, but it was also said out of love: "I love that he's concerned about me making healthy choices." This is an example of emotional granularity at work.

Emotional granularity isn't a matter of simply talking yourself into feeling differently; it's about articulating subtle differences in your experience and strengthening neurological paths that better serve you when life gets tough.

To use emotional granularity for developing better emotional health, Barrett says to start by reinterpreting and recategorizing unpleasant feelings. Instead of getting mad when your toddler pulls off his shoes the second you've wrestled them on to his feet, examine your feelings more closely: Are you self-conscious that you're going to be late? Nervous that others will judge you as a parent for letting your little one run around barefoot? Assess that emotion, and then reframe it.

Shame is never *just* shame. It's the shock of exposure, and fear, when a neighbor casually mentions he can see inside your bedroom curtains. It's a humble remorse when you can't help but break a promise. Shame sneaks in alongside panic, irritation, and guilt when I silence my cousin's call because I'm frantically finishing the dishes before the kids get home from school.

Only after I acknowledge the feeling can I begin to act pragmatically: I can hit send on an email, even though I'm painfully aware it's imperfect. I can stop apologizing for the appearance of my home. I can wear whatever I feel comfortable in, regardless of what others are going to think. I can pack my kid's lunch box with stuff I know they'll actually eat instead of expensive "healthier" options I know will end up in the trash.

Whatever the problem, I know that shame layered on top can make it feel insurmountable. To this day, when I am overwhelmed by difficult feelings, I remind myself of the things I learned years ago in twelve-step programs: all you need to do is take the next right action. From there, more will be revealed.

Progress, Not Perfection

In early sobriety, I grew and learned—sometimes quickly, sometimes slowly—and often from mistakes. "Progress, not perfection" is an oft-used phrase in recovery circles. It's a reminder to focus on smaller achievements instead of an end goal. It encourages folks to accept and enjoy things even if they aren't perfect, and to forgive yourself for your flaws.

I owe my life to the folks I met in twelve step, but I am equally grateful for the harm reduction community, activists fighting for the rights and safety of drug users, people in the sex trades, and other street economies. It is also used by the Disability Rights Movement to defend chronic illnesses and disabilities from the ableist assumption that anyone with a different body can be, and should prefer to be, "better." I'm talking about people who may have no interest in "recovering," who are committed to living in the beauty of their lives no matter how messy they may (appear) to be. Harm reduction is a radical reframing that connects to the principles of shame resilience in its call for radical acceptance. Shame-resilient folks know that judging and finding fault with others obscures the truth: namely, that we are all deserving of respect and that we are not defined by our actions, regardless of our behaviors or conditioning. When it is our habit to meet others with presence and care rather than criticism, we are more likely to meet our own shortcomings with compassion.

Consider this wisdom from activist and author Shira Hassan in her essay "Our Right to Heal: Liberatory Harm Reduction," who describes harm reduction as "a practice steeped in joy."

"I have had several friends who intentionally became pregnant for the sole purpose of getting into rehab or on methadone because pregnant people have access to priority placement," writes Hassan. "If you felt shock or judgment come up when you read that statement, I invite you to answer it with curiosity and compassion. What is life like when becoming pregnant is the best option for someone who wants to get off drugs? What does it mean when the system is so violent that extremes become legal options?"

Harm reduction doesn't blame people for their choices; it contextualizes the choices we make and underscores the fact that we make choices under the condition of structural violence. And all choices are made under these conditions, mind you. The choice of "breast or bottle" may *feel* personal—and on one level, it is. But it is also mitigated by factors beyond our control, including, as bell hooks famously put it, our ubiquitous "Imperialist White Supremacist Heteropatriarchy." A mom might feel pleased with her choice to breastfeed, and proud of all the hard work that went into making that happen, but that choice doesn't make her morally superior. And if she never had to contemplate stealing formula to feed a starving baby, she ought to consider herself lucky.

The practice of radical acceptance—radically accepting myself as I am—requires the radical acceptance of others. It means—above all and no matter what—suspending judgement and seeking to understand.

As part of my recovery work, I started volunteering at OnPoint NYC, called Washington Heights CORNER Project at the time, a syringe exchange program in Upper Manhattan. Around this same time, I also started working for a nonprofit called the NY Writers Coalition, which paid teaching artists like me a very modest stipend to run writing workshops all over the city—from rehabs, hospitals, and homeless shelters to senior centers, after-school clubs, and art galleries.

After six months of volunteering, I applied and received an eight-hundred-dollar grant to fund ten weeks of writing workshops at CORNER Project. Emboldened, I approached other nonprofits directly to offer my services. I began teaching memoir-writing workshops to marginalized communities across the city including drug users, sex worker activists, and LGBTQ+ teens.

Around this same time, I also started teaching memoir-writing for Gotham Writers Workshop. Gotham was my first bread-and-butter job after I lost my position as a schoolteacher—that is, steady work and a reliable paycheck. Anyone who's lived in New York City for any amount of time has heard of Gotham Writers Workshop. They are a creative writing school for everyone. From the whore to the housewife, the convict to the cop—we were all in the same workshop.

"Compassion is not a relationship between the healer and the wounded," Pema Chödrön writes. "It's a relationship between equals. Only when we know our own darkness well can we be present with the darkness of others. Compassion becomes real when we recognize our own shared humanity."

Money Is No Measure of Your Worth

Money shame emerged as the second greatest challenge (behind shame surrounding sex) that the women I spoke to faced. For many, it was a trigger planted young, with parents fighting over custody payments or struggling to make the rent. It was the subject of verbal disagreements or, like sex, was something that was simply never discussed. The women I spoke to expressed concern over how little they earned, especially in comparison to their male partners. ("I did not expect to be a middle-aged lady with such a gross earning history," my one friend lamented, describing herself as "pathetic.") Interviewees felt particularly inadequate if they relied on government assistance or financial support. ("Applying for unemployment and going to DSHS to get back on food stamps, I felt an enormous amount of shame.")

According to US Census Bureau data, there were 37.9 million Americans living in poverty in 2023, and 20.82 million were women. The pandemic put individuals and families at an even greater risk of economic insecurity, due in large part to unprecedented unemployment that has disproportionately affected women and girls.

In the *Huffington Post* essay that ultimately cost me my teaching career, I described sex work as "physically demanding, emotionally taxing, and spiritually bankrupting" and said, "I hope to never again make the choice to trade sex for cash even as I risk my current job and social standing to speak out for an individual's right to do so." When I was underemployed and unemployable in the eyes of many as a consequence of media humiliation, the lure of "easy" money made dancing and escorting loom large. For years, I was so "broke on my ass," as my mom had once so indelicately described it, that I frequently skipped meals and stole rolls of toilet paper from the places where I volunteered. I walked to work instead of taking the train to save two dollars and fifty cents, and I didn't launder my clothes as often as was necessary.

I was ashamed of the rent nonpayment notices frequently taped to my door. Ashamed every time I had to tearfully beg the banker to reverse a fee for insufficient funds. I was exhausted by the mental gymnastics of poverty, of making seven dollars last for a week, "floating" bills, and rationing food. I was ashamed that even though I worked very, very hard—I was very smart and good at my job and willing, at times, to do anything—I barely made ends meet.

Even after I married and was in a dual-income situation, there have been many times when we have struggled to pay our bills. We live paycheck to paycheck and carry a certain amount of debt, largely as a consequence of our special-needs child and the enormous medical and educational burden. Too often too many of us see the systemic injustice as a personal failing. There is no easy, one-size-fits-all antidote to financial insecurity. But burdening the cash strapped with shame—on top of all the material problems that come with economic insecurity—is unconscionable. And unnecessary.

For three years, I taught a weekly workshop at Girls Educational and Mentoring Services, or GEMS, an organization for survivors of commercial sexual exploitation. I was very different from the girls I mentored, but I could relate to the feelings they expressed in their writing. Even those who wanted another way of life find it difficult to transition out of the sex trade, for a host of reasons. Most of the girls I worked with didn't qualify for unemployment and none of them had credit cards or advanced degrees like I did when I transitioned out of sex work. When I watched them go on interviews to retail outlets only to come back disappointed over not getting a minimum-wage job, I could see why many return to "the life." Bearing witness to their stories made me an even fiercer advocate for the decriminalization of sex work. I realized that, even with all my resources and privilege, and my recovery, I (like them) was still incredibly vulnerable to reverting to sex work. The girls at GEMS taught me poverty was nothing to be ashamed of, and that vulnerability was a strength.

There is nothing shameful about being poor—but it's not inherently virtuous either, as some believe. Women, in particular, need to feel more comfortable talking about financial matters. In a 2019 *Washington Post* column, financial expert Jean Chatzky predicted that women will control 75 percent of the discretionary spending around the world by 2029, and that by 2030 women will hold 66 percent of America's wealth. And yet, according to Stefanie O'Connell Rodriguez—money expert and creator of the award-winning newsletter "Too Ambitious"—women are reticent to talk about money and encultured to disavow our power as earners and spenders.

O'Connell Rodriguez looked into research on gendered language around money, including Starling Bank's 2018 study that found 65 percent of money-related articles in women's magazines characterized women as "overspenders" (compared to articles targeted toward men, which emphasize earning money). She presents this information alongside studies that actually compare men's and women's spending habits and find *similar* expenditures. "The shopaholic, the overly 'emotional' young woman practicing 'retail therapy,' the stay-at-home mom spending all of 'her husband's hard earned money,' there's no shortage of cultural archetypes for the female overspender, 'wasting' money on supposedly thoughtless and needless purchases," O'Connell Rodriguez says on Instagram, but these tropes are not grounded in reality.

It must also be noted that—according to O'Connell Rodriguez—for ambitious women, personal success comes with a greater likelihood of relationship stress. "Men are more likely to interpret a partner's success as their own failure," O'Connell Rodriguez says, triggering what she calls the "ambition penalty": "the sum of the social, personal, professional, and financial costs women face for their ambitions."

And about that word "ambition." The concept itself can be shrouded in shame—either because we have too little or because we have too much. In a recent newsletter, journalist Anne Helen Petersen comments on the capitalistic belief that life should be a straight line that keeps pointing up, "despite the inevitability of me eventually getting ill or tired or needing to take a break." We're pushed to do more and achieve more. Heck, even our Apple Watch entices us with a badge if we exercise more than we did the previous month, Petersen laments. But is that kind of continual improvement even realistic? And what happens if—make that *when*—we fall behind? "So much corporate gamification sees that inevitability as a literal failure rather than a part of what it means to be human," she explains.

Petersen is an expert on burnout, which is described as a state of physical, mental, and emotional exhaustion, and is attributed to situations in which the demands persistently outweigh the rewards. At work, women continue to face alarmingly high levels of burnout and stress. An April 2022 study by Deloitte titled *Women at Work 2022: A Global Outlook* found 53 percent of women surveyed said their stress levels were higher than they were a year ago, and that their mental health was poor or very poor. "One third had taken time off due to mental health challenges, yet only 43 percent felt comfortable talking about these challenges on the job," Deloitte US principal Michele Parmelee reported in *Forbes*. Then there's parental burnout, which is associated with depression, anxiety, and increased alcohol consumption, as well as the likelihood for parents to be irritable, get easily angered with their children, and engage in punitive parenting practices (such as yelling, insulting/criticizing, cursing, or spanking).

Whatever its cause, burnout can result in inescapable distress, guilt, and shame—and shame can be a cause of burnout. It's a never-ending cycle, but we don't have to live this way. We can disinvest from this belief and redefine success.

I am by no means immune to the message that my worth is measured by what I've accomplished instead of by something inherent. Even as I consider myself an exceptionally competent and productive individual, I often find myself all worked up over something completely inconsequential that I didn't get done; the thank-you card I forgot to send, the pitch I wrote that was rejected, the dinner I tenderly prepared that even my husband refused to eat. When I find myself in a frenzy over my child's birthday party decorations and getting everything just right—as if the amount of money I pay for a four-year-old's birthday cake is a reflection of my self-worth—I remind myself of all that I've lived through, and all that my friends are living through, and all that I have to be grateful for, and I let that shame go.

Becoming the Love of Your Life

All the while, I kept writing.

Even though it had been my writing that got me in trouble, I did not consider even for a moment that I would stop publishing my stories and sharing my views. It was 2010 and we were in the midst of the confessional essay boom; I was giddy for the chance to tell my story and publish on high-profile platforms very early in my career. Because I had a story they wanted that only I could tell, these editors were willing to teach me the ropes, and I worked with amazing professionals who were extremely patient with me as an inexperienced writer.

Viewed more cynically, you might say these publications were all too eager to monetize my trauma and exploit my naivete and desperation. Writing about sex and sexualizing myself in my writing felt like another kind of sex work, but I lacked the privilege to put myself above it. It was not a question of whether or not it was wise to talk about my alcoholism and sex addiction, to write about my estranged relationship with my father, to write about the time a john ripped me off, and whether or not that counted as "rape" (a story for another book), and other complicated sexual experiences on and off the job. For a long time, it was only a question of "When do you want it by, and what is your rate?" I took whatever platform was given to me, along with the paycheck.

Yes, it was emotional to resurrect the memories. But I did not feel shame in telling these stories aloud. Not anymore. I understood and respected my motivation. I trusted that my sharing would be in service to someone else. I felt as if I was part of a larger movement of women de-individualizing our experiences and getting real for a greater good. And yes, I wanted attention. By now I was unashamed that this is part of my motivation. I wholeheartedly admitted, even then, that I was driven—as is everyone—by a deep desire to be seen, heard, and understood.

I know writers who regret stories they shared. I knew well enough that coming out is not always one hundred percent empowering, and that we're not necessarily being our truest and most authentic self when we're confessing our rawest and most shocking truths. There are times when I reread stories now and cringe at how little I actually knew about myself and the world. But I know what I know now because I was willing to go there then.

Ultimately, it was my early experiences—including teaching elementary school creative writing—that cemented within me a belief in the power of first-person testimony. And yeah, the money I made from my writing aided in my survival, even as every story I wrote and published made the prospect of "normal" employment less and less likely.

"Be nobody's darling," Alice Walker commands. "Be an outcast. / Take the contradictions / Of your life / And wrap around / You like a shawl." This is what I've done, or tried to. For the most part, it's worked out for me.

Becoming a writer, coming clean, and telling the truth of my experience saved my life, even as it further complicated my relationship with my mother.

For a very long time I believed—and suffered from the belief—that if my mother loved me, she would have tried to understand. She would have looked past all the confusion—all the misconceptions about sex work, all the stories she had ever heard about strippers, all the hooker jokes. She would have reached beyond her own fear and prejudice. Had she looked more deeply, she would have seen her daughter. The mother I deserved would have seen through my lies and bore witness to my desperation.

It was by sharing my story, and listening to other women's experiences, that I learned to let go of my shame. For starters, I learned that parents of sex workers don't always automatically reject their children. In an article for *Cosmopolitan* in 2016, adult-film actress Kitty Stryker shared her experience of how the revelation that she was working in the sex industry actually brought her and her mother closer together. When her mother discovered she was making adult movies, Stryker says that she and her mom began to talk more. They started sharing feminist writings on sex work and discussing the ins and outs of ethical porn. They talked about self-care. "My mother didn't yell at me, or talk over me, or dictate to me what I should or shouldn't be doing," Stryker says. "She listened."

Of course, not everybody has such an open relationship with their mothers. And sex workers, current and former, aren't the only ones with tenuous, or nonexistent, maternal relationships, an estrangement that writer Natasha Vargas-Cooper once described in *Jezebel* as "the hardest breakup known to the human heart." Even Stryker concedes in her *Cosmo* piece, "So many people I know can barely talk to their parents about sex, or their queer identity, or their multiple partners, never mind their lives as sex workers."

On my last official day as a teacher, I published an essay on *The Rumpus* about the loss of my career. In it, I talked about the economic hardship I'd experienced as a kid, and how sex work was a means to socioeconomic opportunity. I talked about loss, and grief, and fear. I wrote of financial insecurity, and not knowing what I was going to do now that I'd just been rendered unemployable. I didn't come out and say it, but at that time in my life, I felt tempted to return to the sex industry—which, by then, was work I'd grown to loathe. Instead, I talked about becoming a writer, and what my writing meant to me.

Some days later, my mom sent me an email. In it, she complained I'd painted a "distorted picture of [my] oh so poor childhood." She threatened to discredit me publicly if I continued to embarrass her online or in print.

I wrote her back. I told her what I should have told her years ago, when she first confronted me about the fact that I was dancing: I said that I was sorry she felt embarrassed by my work. I told her that I loved her; I loved her very much—but I would not stop living my truth.

Healing and reconciling who we are after feeling layered violations takes as long as it takes. According to Jessica J. Williams, it is a "deep-rooted unlearning, relearning, and redefining." In her contribution to *You Are Your Best Thing*, "Black Surrender Within the Ivory Tower," Williams describes how she is learning to normalize discomfort, to recognize that feelings of inadequacy are part of the shared human experience, and to get quiet and curious instead of ignoring the feeling or engaging in self-harm. She talks about how she is warm toward herself when feeling pain. She practices mindfulness and takes a "balanced" approach to the feelings that come with life.

"I've had to assure myself that I am not broken or discounted because of what happened to me or because others lack the metrics to appraise my value," Williams writes.

"To be a Black woman in predominantly white spaces for the majority of your days," she continues, "often means affirming yourself or going without affirmation and representation for long stretches of time."

But, as William puts it, "Dangerous is the woman who can give herself what she used to seek from others."

I spent a long time waiting for outside affirmation. I am learning to give myself what I need, and I am surrounding myself with others committed to living similarly.

During this period of my life, I reconnected to the woman I was and the goals I had prior to becoming a sex worker, including a strong desire to start a family. As I looked for a mate to spend my life with, I realized that "I don't have a problem with what you used to do for money, just don't ever talk about it" wasn't good enough. I knew I wanted to discuss my sex work past, the scandal, and everything else—including the fact that I wrote about it all quite frequently—with any potential partner.

In most cases, I saved the big reveal for the fourth date. More than once, after I explained my situation, a look of worry washed over my dates' faces. These were the "good" guys who'd conflate sex work with sex trafficking and would assume all sex work to be tantamount to abuse.

On at least one date, the opposite happened: the guy was obviously titillated, drooling for details about my former occupation as if he'd stumbled upon a living, breathing character out of a Penthouse Forum letter. I wasn't ashamed of my past, but at that time in my life I wasn't necessarily proud of it either—and I definitely wasn't looking for someone else to use it to objectify me. What had been a pleasant evening of getting to know each other better turned into an invasive, uncomfortable Q and A. Instead of inviting him up at the end of the date, as I could tell he was expecting, I sent him on his way.

When I was coming of age, sex-positive feminism was an antidote to anti-sex-industry feminists who placed pornography and sex work at the center of women's oppression, but the sex-positive movement's reductive messaging that all consensual sex is "healthy" led me and other women to accept mediocre sex as permissible just because we'd said yes.

Single at thirty, I found myself part of a new movement of women insisting upon more satisfying sexual encounters—intimacies that are not only consensual but free from violence, nonexploitative, safe, protected from unwanted pregnancy, and pleasurable. Clementine Morrigan has written brilliantly on her Instagram account about why many women struggle with directness when it comes to sex. "Due to being socialized into sexual passivity, and due to past experiences where their sexual and bodily autonomy was overridden," Morrigan contends that a lot of us have trouble saying no. But to quote *Pleasure Activism* author adrienne maree brown, "Your strong and solid no makes way for your deep, authentic yes."

I would not say that love became a requirement for physical intimacy, but my sex life improved dramatically when I reframed the act from, well, an act. I stopped performing some idea of "sexy" and started asking myself what I found desirable. I stopped settling for folks just because they liked me and started pursuing people I liked back. I started thinking more critically what it means to actually like someone—people I could be honest with, women and men who shared my values and whom I could trust. This kind of reclamation flies in the face of the ways sexual pleasure is understood in our society. We live in a world where women are harassed and abused on television and in the movies and these acts are sexualized and romanticized. A world where people's idea of "manliness" perpetuates domination, homophobia, and aggression. Imagine being a loved one of one of his victims and reading the *Washington Post*'s description of serial killer Gary Leon Ridgway: "He was nothing if not pragmatic. He liked killing prostitutes, he said, because they were easy to pick up, they were slow to be reported missing, and, if they had any money on them, they ended up paying him for their own murder. Occasionally he would have sex with decaying corpses." In a world where the bodies of women being harmed is served as entertainment and "news," while the dangerous men responsible are humanized, violence and love become entwined. It is no wonder women frequently struggle to know what we desire.

I didn't give him my last name on our first date, but Arran had figured it out after our initial meeting and googled me. Still, he stayed quiet on the subject of my sex work past until I brought it up. By then, I'd made it clear what I was looking for in a relationship—respect, commitment, and honesty—and he'd made it clear he wanted the same.

When I finally worked up the courage to broach the topic of my former occupation, Arran put me at ease. He told me something equally personal about him to even the playing field, and the conversation moved on. On the issue of sex work, Arran was more or less neutral. Sure, he leaned toward the progressive position that whatever a person wanted to do with their body was their choice; he also understood that, when it came to sex work, "choice" could be complicated. Most importantly, he came to the conversation with an abundant awareness of all he didn't know. He let me be the expert; at the same time, he didn't demand that I educate him.

Sex can be a means of communicating, a source of pleasure and connection, a way to unburden ourselves from everything impressed upon us both as parents and caregivers, men and women, and a way to reinhabit our bodies. When it comes to dating and relationships, we've all got baggage. What works in my marriage is that Arran and I are both teachable, and we are committed to doing the work. Neither of us demand the other to be perfect, only that we both remain open and willing to learn.

A year later, we made it official. In a white lace dress I found on an Anthropologie clearance rack and a homemade flower crown, carrying a bouquet I picked up that morning from our local bodega, I passed as the picture of a traditional bride—but for my half-sleeve tattoo and my provocative history. In front of fifty or so invited guests, Arran promised to be communicative, to stay present, to make me laugh, to make me coffee every morning. I promised to always keep him guessing, to keep growing spiritually, to call on him, to answer his call, and to be a partner in every sense of the word.

7

Happier Endings

We Are More Than Monogamy and Mothering

Pregnant for the first time, I had no idea what was "normal," so I did what most of us do when we have a question: I googled it. Every night after powering through a day of nausea, fatigue, and malaise, I'd search the number of weeks I was to find out what was happening inside me.

Scrolling past stock photos of conventionally attractive white women with perfect skin, perfect smiles, the perfect office-ready wardrobe, thin but for their bump, which was perfectly round and smooth, nary a stretch mark in sight, I absorbed the expectation placed on pregnant people. In society's imagination of pregnancy, there was no linea nigra, no pile of laundry in the background, no existential despair. With a little staging and the right filter, I fit right in.

The conditions were optimal: my pregnancy was planned and wanted, getting pregnant had been relatively easy, and everything up until delivery went without complication. My husband is emotionally supportive, and we are financially secure and relatively privileged in nearly every way. It's perhaps no wonder then, I enjoyed all aspects of my pregnancy.

While the majority of the country mourned the 2016 election results, my husband and I prepared for what was promised to be the greatest joy of our lives. Even as my ordinarily athletic body had taken on the shape of a fertility statue, and cellulite visibly dimpled my arms, I happily indulged in my pregnancy cravings, downing pickles by the jarful and sending my husband out for doughnuts at eleven at night. On social media, I posted filtered photos from not one but two babymoons: a weekend at a dog-friendly bed-and-breakfast upstate followed by four days on a beach.

Divorced from all this was the idea that the thing swimming inside of me was actually a baby—a life, not the piece of fruit or vegetable the articles I read on the internet compared it to. I had no idea how dramatically my life was about to change. Today I recognize how the spectacle of pregnancy did nothing to prepare me for motherhood—that, in fact, it did the opposite: how "bump dates" and baby showers and stroller porn and the whole pregnancy industrial complex conditions women like me to be complacent about a pregnant person's utter lack of rights. Being an educated, critically thinking woman, a part of me must have realized that the hollow idealization of motherhood was no substitute for freedoms or entitlements, but I remained willfully ignorant.

As a former sex worker, I thought marriage and motherhood would usher in a social acceptance beyond anything I'd ever experienced.

Marriage and motherhood was a new adventure I didn't want to corrupt with cynicism. But spoiler alert: there is no happy ending, not really, not even if you meet and marry "the one." Instead, relationships have ups and downs, couples disagree, and marriage is often harder work than we're taught to anticipate. For women in particular, it is normal to experience profound relationship dissatisfaction, particularly after the birth of your first child. One notable study led by world-renowned researchers and clinical psychologists Drs. John and Julie Gottman found that most couples experience a precipitous drop in happiness during the first three years as new parents, on par with death of a spouse. And in a society that supposedly celebrates parenthood—motherhood, specifically—above all else, the shame of even acknowledging that it might not be all you expected can be crushing.

I didn't know to expect all this when I said, "I do." I hadn't heard about things like invisible labor or the mental load. No one warned me of perinatal depression. Instead, when I felt dissatisfied, I blamed myself. Then—as we commonly do in an attempt to escape our own self-conscious feelings—I blamed the person I love, even though the oppressive systems we labor under were no more my husband's fault than they were mine.

The Reality of "Having It All"

Georgia's life on social media looks pretty damn perfect. She's a working mom, the polished and professional type that goes to an office in beautiful silk blouses and pressed linen pants. She's got a flawless manicure in spite of the fact that she's mothering young kids. She's got a full social calendar, and she can somehow balance cocktails with coworkers and nights out with the girls, all while still bringing a home-cooked dish to the birthday or graduation party. Her life is swelling with family and friends.

When it's just her and me, Georgia keeps it real about being unreal: "This world and especially social media got us thinking that other people got their shit together and are so happy. LIES!

"Look at me," she continues. "I look like this perfect happy family, married for almost twenty years with three beautiful kids. I get so many compliments on how beautiful my family is and how in love my husband and I look. If you ask me, I feel like I've been in survival mode for the past decade," Georgia confesses. "Yeah, I have a lovely home, amazing kids, an awesome husband who loves me, but I am still not happy. I am going through depression but here I am faking that shit, just waiting for my kids to get older and I can finally start living my life."

Like Georgia, my life on social media looks pretty damn perfect! I am just another thin, blonde, white woman, a happily married Karen with a handsome husband and two young, incredibly cute kids. I know how to signal all the visual clues that my husband and I are highly educated and professionally successful, from our lovely home in Westchester, a wealthy suburb one hour from the city of New York, to photos of our frequent vacations and dinners out. (You don't see that many of those trips and meals are comped in exchange for travel-writing essays, or the meltdown that preceded those highly edited photos of children bouncing on enormous white hotel beds.) On Instagram there are no outstanding Con Ed bills or awkward, ongoing feuds with your in-laws. It's all tomatoes homegrown in the garden and enormous birthday cakes decked out in buttercream.

Even though we're smart enough to know better, when it comes to marriage and motherhood, imaginary ticking clocks and the desire for normalcy spur us on. According to Gallup, 69 percent of people have been married at some point in their lives, down from 80 percent in 2006. The iconic nuclear family describes just 18 percent of today's households, and an increasing number of women are choosing to be single or are feeling comfortable with their choice to live child-free. And yet, the word "spinster" is still imbued with pity and misogyny. Even as a 2020 Pew Research study finds that dating has gotten more dangerous and difficult, the pressure to find a partner and have children is real. Many would still insist you're not complete without a family—defined as a partner and kids.

Where do we get these narrow, outdated concepts? The modern idea of "having it all" may have originated with Helen Gurley Brown's book *Having It All: Love, Success, Sex, Money, Even if You're Starting with Nothing* (although Brown's "all" didn't include the kids part of the equation—she was famously child-free throughout her life). In a 2015 *New York Times* piece, Jennifer Szalai traces the history of the phrase "having it all" and how it's come to be viewed in the popular imagination (and weaponized against women). "Having it all" has become "a burden and a cliché" and "a charming artifact from a more hopeful time," Szalai writes.

Since *Having It All*'s publication in 1982 (I was shocked by this date, mistakenly thinking it was a *Mad Men*–era concept rather than one concurrent with the go-go '80s!), Szalai says the phrase "having it all" has been twisted to describe this fictitious woman many of us strive to be, someone who could effortlessly balance the demands of career with the demands of motherhood—"an equilibrium that, as the economy continues to grind its gears," Szalai says, "feels increasingly out of reach."

Szalai's piece explains how the phrase was falsely equated with feminism and underscores that Brown's vision of "it all" never included a woman having kids: "Only six of the 462 pages of *Having*

It All mention them," Szalai writes, "and Brown has a hard time disguising her suspicion that children aren't so seamlessly integrated into her program.

"Admitting her own lack of firsthand knowledge on the subject," Szalai continues, "she quotes several of her time-starved mother-friends as authorities and sounds mildly flummoxed that anyone would willingly undertake such an endeavor: 'Isn't that a hard sell if you ever *heard* one?'"

The work it takes to manage the home is vast, and as we know, the lion's share of that work falls on women. So let's talk about it: the burden of managing the home and taking responsibility for each and every easily discounted but indispensable, under-the-radar task that keeps a family's life afloat. How do women do it? Why are we still expected to? And is there any remedy for the crushing shame we feel when we fall short?

How, in the year of our Lord 2024, is it still a woman's job to keep the home well-stocked with everything from toilet paper and paper towels to groceries and durable goods? We organize the social calendar, arrange playdates, buy presents, and bake gluten-free brownies for the school fundraiser. Frequently, it's moms that do the schlepping, shuttling children to and from daycare, after-school activities, and doctors' appointments.

Let's talk about how all these individual tasks have a number of invisible steps and carry an incalculable mental load—that is, the cognitive effort involved in managing your household. Cooking, for example, is so much more than cooking. It's taking inventory of what's in the fridge and pantry, looking up recipes and planning the meal, making a grocery list, going to the store, shopping, bringing it all home, putting it away, defrosting the meat, marinating the vegetables, remaking the leftovers into tomorrow's lunches. Eve Rodsky writes about this phenomenon of "invisible work" in her book *Fair Play*, saying, "*invisible* because it may be unseen and unrecognized by our partners, and also because those of us who do it may not count or even acknowledge it as work . . . despite the fact that it costs us real time and significant mental and physical effort with no sick days or benefits."

It's time to raise our own and each other's critical awareness about the fact that the majority of this labor falls on women. We know from experience that care work is still largely seen as naturally female, invisible, and underpaid if it's compensated at all. New terms are constantly emerging to describe the unappreciated things we do, like the term "kin keeping," a word to describe the endless creating and maintaining of relationships that falls on women and that families rely on to survive. When the other moms and I swap outgrown clothes or organize a meal train for a neighbor going through a medical emergency, or when I am having lunch with another mom who has a child that shares the same diagnosis as my son, she and I are not simply socializing—we're doing vital work for our family.

Let's talk about how all of this is taken for granted, and how we even take ourselves for granted. How we don't value the labor in packing our kids' school lunches or recognize the strengths or skills it takes to advocate for our children at drop-off. We settle for a measly thirty minutes of "me time" when dads get double. We undervalue our own contributions—the steam-cleaned sofa, the schlepping, the hard conversation we had with our kid—and dwell on what we didn't get done.

All day long, minute to minute, I feel the pressure to work, and to not work but instead take care of my family. Around every corner, there's another irritating reminder of something that I haven't done—from the voicemail from my kids' dentist telling me I have an appointment I haven't rescheduled since before COVID to the light in my car letting me know an oil change is overdue.

I asked my friends on social media to be honest: "Is 'having it all' something you still strive for?"

"I don't love this about myself but yes," Raven admits. "I value the perception of 'having it all' even if that means that at times I am wading deeply mentally challenging and physically exhausting waters to pull 'it all' off."

"I like the mantra 'you can have it all, but not at once,'" says Toni. "Like the year I got divorced, moved into my own place, got a new better paying job, and was solo parenting five nights a week—maybe that's not the year I experiment with new recipes or get really toned. Maybe it's not the year I join a book club. I see some of those things in my future, maybe even my near future, but I'm not there yet. And I definitely feel a lot of pressure."

"I'm sure the right answer is no—because, duh," says Freda. "But I have absolutely been indoctrinated to believe that if I make smart decisions and work hard enough, I can somehow be a mother and a writer and a wife and a caretaker to aging parents and a friend and an intellectual woman-of-the-world. So while I know that it is obviously impossible (at least for those of us who are not wealthy), it's also something I continue to feel a tremendous amount of pressure to achieve—and shame about when I inevitably fail."

All these women are, objectively, killing it. They're heroic. They're wonderful. Still, shame finds a way.

The Promise of Happiness

Four years and thirty-something first dates after I lost my teaching career, I reinvented myself yet again when I met and married my husband, Arran. A little over a year later, my first child was born. On the surface, I traded six-inch plastic heels, rhinestone chokers, and dates-for-pay for playdates, sweatshirts, and yoga pants (never mind I'd long ago stopped going to the gym). Except for my provocative history, I became in every way your typical stay-at-home mom: relatively satisfied, grateful, #blessed . . . but also bored, burnt out, under constant surveillance by literally everyone and yet utterly invisible, frequently mom-shamed and, consequentially, ashamed, just as I'd felt when I sold sex.

Without a doubt, the sex industry—and women who participate in it—are uniquely misunderstood, but modern motherhood, too, is cloaked in misconception. In popular culture, mothers are caricatured as either magical or miserable. We are, as writer Jude Doyle once observed for *Elle*, "the glowing, selfless Madonna who spends every minute in rapt contemplation of her child's perfection" or else a mother is a "harried, frazzled, three-days-without-a-shower woman who tromps through life in sweatpants covered in baby urine and milky spit-up." Housewives, in particular, are painted as powerless servants to their husbands, who malevolently exploit them—or else, just like sex workers, we are cast as villains, penned into sacrificing so much for the sake of our families but somehow still negligent and immoral for not sacrificing enough.

In her book *Small Animals: Parenthood in the Age of Fear*, Kim Brooks explores the animus aimed at mothers. Says Brooks, "We're contemptuous of mothers who have no choice but to work, but also of mothers who don't need to work and still fail to fulfill an impossible ideal of selfless motherhood. You don't have to look very hard to see the common denominator."

Becoming a stay-at-home mom had not originally been my plan. In my mind, as for many, it was synonymous with being a housewife—unemployed and financially dependent on one's husband, and without any meaningful responsibilities (never mind the extraordinary labor of caring for one's kids). At best, the stay-at-home mom is cast as a natural martyr, devoted—nay, obsessed—with her family. At worst, she's painted as a lazy, self-indulgent woman who spends her idle days lunching with fellow unemployed mommies or frittering away her hardworking husband's salary on shopping. We are disparaged as anti-feminist and assumed to be economically privileged, never mind that Institute for Family Studies reports that stay-at-home moms are represented in every section of the tax bracket, with the highest concentrations hovering around the uppermost 5 percent of earners as well as the lowest 25 percent.

Above all, we are considered fortunate and expected to be happy with our lot in life.

In *The Promise of Happiness*, Sara Ahmed says the image of the happy housewife that populated magazines and newspapers in the United States and the United Kingdom in the 1950s and '60s still retains incredible sway over public imagination. Ahmed cites conservative radio commentator Darla Shine's 2005 book *Happy Housewives* as just one example of a new generation of bloggers who present the housewife lifestyle as one of leisure, comfort, and ease.

Such blogs, Ahmed observes, "typically include recipes, tips on doing housework, thoughts on mothering, as well as belief statements that register the happy housewife as an important social role and duty that must be defended, as if the speech act ('I am a happy housewife') is itself a rebellion against a social orthodoxy." Shine's book, in particular, Ahmed writes, "calls for us to return to a certain kind of life, as if this was the kind of life that women gave up in embracing feminism: [Shine's] fantasy of the happy housewife is as much a white bourgeois fantasy of the past, a nostalgia for a past that was never possible as a present for most women, let alone being available in the present."

Two decades since Shine warned us what might happen if we make our desires and even our own happiness conditional on the happiness of others, Millennial women all over TikTok are rejecting the "have it all" nonsense and opting to focus on being a good mom and wife. But British researcher Shani Orgad cautions that media constructions of the stay-at-home mom who has opted out of the workplace as a personal choice obfuscate the complex factors that shape our choice—everything from the paucity of affordable, quality childcare and the untold costs of breastfeeding to a husband's demanding and prioritized career. Sara Petersen's book *Momfluenced* is a more recent look at the momfluencer landscape, a world in which the stay-at-home mom is increasingly being recast as an empowered (some might even say feminist) choice. Petersen's work calls attention to the unspoken fact that many of these so-called stay-at-home moms are working for money—even and particularly the ones garnering huge follower counts by espousing a "traditional" view of wives as mothers and homemakers. All those product lines and sponsored social media posts? That woman is getting paid for that work. She is contributing to her family financially, on top of everything else.

"Mothering is overstimulating, overwhelming, stressful, isolating, and disappointing," says content creator Libby Ward. "Messes we didn't make. Meals nobody ate. Plans that ended in tears. It's not the *work* that's the hardest part, but how pointless it can sometimes feel."

"I think my favorite part of being a mother has been sacrificing my body, career, mental stability, and physical appearance to wait on them hand and foot. Only to be met with 'YOU DON'T DO ANY-THING FOR ME' when I ask them to pick up a fruit snack wrapper," quips writer Scarlett Longstreet on Twitter.

I mean, *really*: When you thought of motherhood, is this what you imagined?

"It was such a journey for me to become a mother," Ryan says. "I felt like less of a woman when I couldn't get pregnant or carry a child to full term."

Instead of relief and a sense of belonging after she adopted her son, Ryan says the isolation continued.

"I'm always watching other moms and thinking maybe they are a better mom than me," Ryan says. "Maybe they play with their kids constantly and don't ever just want to be left alone. And look how that mom is so comfortable with her child or children climbing or running—why can't I be like that?"

Penny also struggles with comparisons: "I still want to telegraph 'cool mom' in the ways I style my hair and clothes. I think it's really important to me to feel like I'm not quite a total suburban mom (even though I really am on paper)."

Penny adds that she's gained a lot of true healing and peace from learning how to parent gently. At the same time, she admits, "I always feel like there's more to do if I'm 'doing it right.'"

A parenting style that encourages us to treat our children with understanding, empathy, and respect; to listen to them; and to validate their feelings—what could possibly be wrong with this? "In theory, [gentle parenting] is lovely," Amil Niazi writes for *The Cut,* but "in practice, most of us are exhausted, confused, and looking for an approach that isn't quite so hard on us parents." As it is, Niazi continues, "I'm constantly trying to figure out how to responsibly, kindly and expertly manage both my kids' outsize emotions and my own in increasingly trying situations," admitting that her desire to be a good, gentle parent often means "swallowing any semblance of frustration and emotion I might be feeling."

"In all my different roles there's always a feeling of 'I should be better," Alicia says. "A better wife, a better mom, a cleaner household. I should be more thin, more organized, I should exercise more. But also I should be more mindful. I should give myself grace."

How Did We Get Here?

Before we had a child, my husband and I did our best to split the household work equally. I insisted that we contribute fifty-fifty to our family budget, even though I made less than a third of Arran's salary. It never occurred to me that, because we didn't start off as equal, this wasn't equitable. I did not account for the fact that he didn't have student loans and I did, that he had savings and owned stocks, and that he had parents he had borrowed money from when times got tough. I didn't recognize my husband's advantages, I only saw that he was financially secure (read: *responsible*), and I was not.

Shame resilience would ask that we investigate the social conditions that created our circumstances, so let's do that. Arran makes more money than I do because he's always done traditionally masculine work. A fine-arts painter by education, he worked as a security guard at the Metropolitan Museum of Art and then at the U.K.

Mission to the U.N., where he Good Will Hunted his way into a white-collar position on the other side of the desk. Today he works in the tech side of digital communications and multimedia—i.e., a STEM field, which is dominated by men.

Whereas all my life, I've done "women's work." Social work, teaching children, working as a stripper, and having sex for cash—though not all traditional jobs—are all jobs traditionally held by women. Even the sort of personal, sometimes confessional, writing I had settled into by then was derided as "women's writing." With the exception of sex work, these jobs were underpaid or not paid at all. They're considered unskilled and are extremely undervalued by society.

By the time Arran and I met, I had stopped looking for a "real" job and surrendered to freelancing. I had come to terms with the fact that I would never teach children again in a traditional setting. My past would *always* be an issue, I realized, a prediction that has more or less come true.

As a freelance writer and writing instructor, I am one of a growing number of people participating in the "gig economy," the term used to describe workers who are self-employed and hired on demand for single projects or assignments. There are obvious advantages to this approach to earning money, for mothers especially: theoretically, workers like me have the freedom and flexibility to take projects that interest us, and to work when we want. We can refuse work and take off hours, days, or even weeks at will. As opposed to a salary, what you earn is proportionate to how often you work—meaning the harder you hustle, the more money you make.

But sometimes no matter how hard you hustle, you find yourself between jobs. A lot of the labor of freelancing—including the hard work of finding work—goes unpaid. Before I had kids, I took these challenges on the chin. Even before Oscar was born, I suffered through debilitating pregnancy symptoms that I barely let register. I tried to carry on as normal, even when the challenges knocked me out.

Anne Helen Petersen nailed it in a 2022 article for *Businessweek*, "The Work-From-Home Revolution Is Also a Trap for Women." She called moms like me "one-woman safety nets." In spite of all the advantages of and reasons we love the flexibility of working from home, Petersen says, there's a catch: "That additional flexibility opens up a space, and that space is quickly filled with responsibilities that were once more equally distributed: between partners in a relationship, but also between citizens and the society of which they are a part."

When I brought up the question of work-life balance, my Facebook group of women freelancers lit up with horror stories:

> Between sick days, snow days, and school breaks, I am the one who has the kids while my partner leaves for work. It's a lot of pressure to make money, be available, take care of the house and all of the cooking and cleaning that goes with it. Yet, we are still living paycheck to paycheck. To make more money, I need to work. But to work, I need time—which is nearly impossible when my first priority is to take care of the kids. It's an awful cycle. My partner is super supportive, but since her job pays the bills and carries our health insurance, this is the way it goes for now.

> It's not so much the stress of working and balancing it all, as it is the stress of wondering if it's going to be a day that falls apart: Will the school-aged kid get sick today? Will the baby be clingy? Am I going to be able to focus and be productive,

or will it be an off day? My work time is finite, whereas my partner can just call and say, "Hey, I have to stay late tonight." Can you imagine the luxury?!

My husband works from home and feels zero compunction to clean or do anything other than work until he has to pick up the kids from school. I work from home sometimes and am always starting dinner in between meetings or grading or writing. The other day my husband was literally napping on the couch when I got home from teaching and then asked me what's for dinner when I walked in the house.

In spite of our intentions and egalitarian beliefs, it's not unusual for heterosexual couples to fall into the roles experts describe as gender typical, even those without children. Sociologist Pamela Smock found women tend to perform chores that take place inside the home and are more likely to be responsible for tasks that are routine, accomplished daily, and closely associated with childcare—things like meal preparation, house cleaning, laundry, and cleaning up after meals.

Of course, there are exceptions—my husband, for example, is often better at remembering to text thank you—and men have their own list of things to do. For the most part, it's still Arran's job to take out the garbage, and only he knows what day of the month to drag the cardboard or mixed recycling to the curb. For years, he "manned" the thermostat, cared for the pets, mowed the lawn, and did a million other things I undoubtedly discounted in addition to commuting three hours a day, often early in the morning or late at night, to work a full-time job.

Undoubtedly though, I did more. And *then* we had Oscar.

Eight months pregnant, I started looking into daycares and came to the damning realization that I was earning only slightly more than what our then-hypothetical childcare would cost. After the baby was born, it would make no financial sense for me to continue working full time, I concluded, especially so long as I wanted to breastfeed.

Rather than hiring a nanny or sending our son off to daycare, I told Arran I'd handle the childcare, along with all the housework and other familial responsibilities. Instead of paying a team of professionals, I reasoned, we'd pay me.

That day, while my husband was away at the office, I sat down and added up the hours I'd work each week and multiplied that by fifteen dollars, an hourly wage we might pay an inexperienced sitter (assuming we could find one). I then divided that number in half—after all, childcare was as much my expense as it was my husband's—and subtracted this figure from what I owed the family budget.

There was some difference to be made up—around $1,200, or half of what I was contributing before I became a stay-at-home mom—and I had to earn any money for my personal needs as well (things like clothes, coffees out, and gifts), so it was understood I wasn't surrendering my career entirely. At the time, completely unaware of what I was in for as a new mother, I thought of working in addition to caregiving as a plus, instead of anticipating it as a further, crushing pressure.

While the arrangement may have been unorthodox, the basics of our situation are in no way unique. The United States has one of the highest wage gaps between men and women, the least-generous benefits for its citizens, and the lowest public commitment to caregiving of any industrialized nation in the West. As a result, American mothers are often compelled to drop out of the workforce. In 2016 alone, the National Survey of Children's Health reports "an estimated two million parents of children aged five and younger had to quit a job, not take a job, or significantly change their job because of problems with childcare." While the problem of childcare affects both men and women, the fact that women are still the primary caregivers means it disproportionately falls on us moms.

It's not this way everywhere. In Sweden, for example, parents receive extra tax credits to defray the cost of child-rearing, plus access to regulated, subsidized daycare facilities that stay open from 6:30 in the morning until 6:30 at night. Similar programs exist in Denmark and Finland. In Germany, every child over the age of one has the legal right to a space in a public daycare facility, a mandate taken so seriously that parents can sue the government for failing to provide childcare.

While other nations make supporting mothers and children a priority, American families like mine are left to figure it out for ourselves. And feel the burden of shame when things slip through the cracks.

"It Was All on Me"

Initially, in spite of and to a certain extent because of what society says, I took enormous pride in my job as a stay-at-home mom, just as I'd taken a certain satisfaction from sex work. Thanks to stripping, in particular, I knew how to hustle. Days sped past, a blur of momming and chores. When I wasn't singing Oscar songs, reading him books, or changing his diaper, I was doing the dishes, making the bed, folding laundry, or preparing meals. Full-time parenting was nonstop from eight until six, at which point my husband came home and we'd split the "second shift." With my husband's help, I'd get the baby fed, bathed, and put to bed, then feed myself and my husband before passing out at the start of my favorite television program.

And where in that schedule does one find time for writing? Certainly, I'd fallen for the pervasive myth that I could somehow squeeze a full-time job around a nap schedule. I didn't respect that creative work requires full concentration. I had also underestimated the physical, mental, and psychological toll of giving birth and caring for an infant.

As Oscar dropped naps and grew more mobile, I got even less done. Deadlines whizzed past and private students lost patience when I prioritized the needs of my demanding toddler. Instead of responding to my agent, editing my students' essays, and following up on outstanding invoices, I was paying bills, planning meals, and picking up toys.

As one can imagine, all this pressure had a huge impact on my physical, mental, and emotional health. Stay-at-home moms—particularly those of us who have internalized the misconception that we are necessarily privileged, i.e., "lucky" to "get to" stay home and "not have to work"—are at heightened risk for parental burnout. A Gallup poll of more than 60,000 US women interviewed in 2012 revealed that more stay-at-home moms (SAHMs) report experiencing sadness or anger in their day than moms who work outside the home. According to another study out of Arizona State University, SAHMs who would prefer to be working reported the lowest levels of personal fulfillment and the highest levels of emptiness and loneliness, compared to stay-at-home moms who would not prefer to be working and to mothers who worked.

Lest you think the solution is to surrender to a full-time job out of the home, know that working moms are at risk of parental burn-out, too. A 2022 study out of the Ohio State University found 66 percent of working parents met the criteria for parental burnout, and that females are one of the groups at greater risk. Anxiety in the parent, having children with either diagnosed anxiety or ADHD, and parental concern that their children may have an undiagnosed mental health disorder show the strongest associations with working parental burnout. A separate survey commissioned by CVS Health in 2022 found that nearly half of all working mothers had been di-agnosed with anxiety or depression (compared to 28 percent of the general population and 25 percent of their coworkers without kids).

Prior to becoming a parent, Tianna felt excited. "Becoming a mother was something I'd looked forward to all my life. I was also really terrified," she admits. "I was terrified to tell my family, mostly because at the time my husband and I weren't married. I had also just started my job the year prior, and felt nervous, not telling my employer as well."

Tianna ended up having a fair amount of health complications during this first pregnancy, she says, and was put on bedrest eight weeks before her daughter was born. Days prior to a scheduled C-section, she was in the hospital for high blood pressure. Then, as they were getting her ready for surgery, Tianna had felt a sudden, over-whelming sense of panic.

"I wasn't entirely sure what was even happening. I felt hot all over, my body was vibrating, my head was spinning, and I started breath-ing very hard. It felt as if I couldn't catch my breath."

An alarm sounded, and residents filled the room. "I was basically half naked in this hospital gown about to go into surgery having an anxiety attack."

After giving birth, Tianna was overcome with self-blame. Even now, when she reflects back, she takes responsibility for how hard it was. She says, "I've had depression all my life since I was a teenager, so I really should have better anticipated the changing hormones and impact that had."

She blames her pregnancy complications on the fact that "I was eating so much, giving in to cravings and definitely not taking care of myself." She speculates now that her eating habits somehow caused her daughter's crankiness and overall disposition as a newborn, "which no one has even said."

As a newborn, her daughter cried a lot and was very hard to comfort. "I had to rock her vigorously to calm her and when I tried to put her down, she would wake up and scream. I was exhausted, and I remember thinking, 'I understand why people shake babies,' which I know is a horrible thing to say and I felt horrible for thinking it."

Her partner tried to help, Tianna says, "however, there was only so much he could do." She was breastfeeding exclusively, and the baby "really wanted to nurse all the time and it was the only time we all seemingly got rest, so it was all on me."

Tianna says she felt exhausted, physically tired, isolated, and as if her body was not her own anymore.

At her six-week postpartum appointment, her obstetrician gynecologist administered a test to rate depression symptoms and she ranked high: "I was like, I'm going to be brave and tell her that I have these horrible intrusive thoughts about falling down the stairs and me throwing her down the stairs.

"I said, please don't call CPS on me, and she said: That's totally normal. It's postpartum anxiety."

Tianna was prescribed Zoloft. Medication helped. But mothering, in addition to full-time work outside of the home, was still a struggle.

As her family grew, the struggle intensified. After the birth of her second child, she says, "I felt exhausted, anxious, strung out, and frankly, I was mean and not the parent I wanted to be with my kids. I had zero patience and didn't have the time I wanted to spend with them," Tianna says.

"I think the worst I felt in terms of parental burnout was during the pandemic. Working from home and being home with them all day and night was really wearing on me. My partner was an essential worker so he was gone each day as well.

"I felt like I was responsible for everything. Cooking, cleaning, their schoolwork, my schoolwork, but probably most exhausting was feeling like I had to entertain and enrich them all day. It was really hard. I felt like I was drowning and going insane."

Tianna recalls the day she had, as she puts it, a complete meltdown, screaming at her then-toddler for making a mess: "I realized I was putting far too much pressure on myself.

"I just wanted to cry and be by myself, which was never an option during the quarantine."

Working outside the home or not, research finds that parents who burn out are often those who looked forward to parenthood the most and who give it their all. In a few words: overcommitted, overzealous parents. I was one of these mothers, as were so many of my friends. Competent women achieving what we imagined would be a dream, starting a family and forwarding our careers. We feel grateful; we are also demoralized, exhausted, enraged, resentful, enduring, and ashamed—waiting for the moment when we'll finally get to catch our breath.

Minding the Gap

"Doing everything related to childcare and housekeeping seemed demanding yet reasonable when I was not working," Heather tells me. "I cleaned the house, supervised and educated the children, shopped for all necessities and gifts. It was all me—planning all appointments and parties, organizing the scheduling of all the trips, packing the bags, planting and harvesting our garden, and basically everything else.

"Now that I am back to working full-time as a teacher," Heather continues, "it is more than I can gracefully manage in the short nights and weekends."

Heather describes her husband as a fantastic partner who is willing to take on more household responsibilities.

"Still," Heather says, "and I don't know if it is me or him or both of us who have preconceived notions of what should be my responsibility versus his—but I just tend to do everything that needs to be done."

On reflection, she admits, "I definitely have a hard time watching him do things that do not meet my standards, or letting him do things that I am particular about."

As an example, she shares the time she asked her husband to take a sick child to the doctor:

"He came home with a prescription for amoxicillin for our two-year-old the day before Thanksgiving," Heather says. "Both of us are allergic to amoxicillin, so I've never given it to my children, and I didn't want to try it out on a major holiday. I remind the doctor of our allergies whenever I take our children for sick visits, but it didn't occur to him.

"I also don't think my house is clean unless I clean it," admits Heather. "So I end up with too much of the load."

This sentiment was echoed in the comments on economist and author Emily Oster's Instagram post discussing a 2023 Pew Research Center study confirming what we all already knew: Pew surveyed heterosexual couples about their time use and income, and found that despite incomes becoming more equal between spouses, women are still doing the bulk of household tasks. Even when the wife is the primary earner, she still does more of the household work—18.1 versus 12.2 hours per week, Oster says, a difference that is very similar to what we see when both partners earn around the same amount. Commenters lamented:

> So if my priority is to not have a filthy home and to have tasks completed in a timely manner (like emptying the dishwasher, wiping surfaces, general tidying) and his isn't, what can be done? I'm so tired of the resentment over this issue, but not sure what the solution is.

> I get this about dinner. I'm the only one who cares if dinner is well balanced.

> I spend more time organizing and picking up our kids' toys than my husband. Not saying that my husband won't help if I ask and he certainly will help supervise our kids cleaning up,

but I care that toys are cleaned up every night, so I make sure it's done whereas his mindset is "They are just going to get them out again tomorrow." He certainly makes more of an effort knowing I like them picked up but his standards aren't where mine are.

Years ago, I would have commiserated. My husband, Arran, does not care if a room is "reset" just as soon as the children are finished playing in it. He is not bothered by a smudge or smear or smell. When I'm in charge, there are no smudges or smears. The house smells of Fabuloso, scented candles, and Certified Naturally Grown specialty cut flowers from the local, small-scale organic farm.

For years, I controlled Dad's household responsibilities and, to a certain extent, his interactions with his children because I didn't trust him to do it "correctly." The term for this is "maternal gate-keeping," and this internalized belief, that we are the only people capable of providing care for our children, comes part and parcel with the perfect mother trope.

The Center for Social and Cultural Psychology, in Belgium, describes maternal gatekeeping as a pattern of behavior of restricting our partner's involvement in household and childcare by "guarding" the management of these tasks, doing tasks ourselves, setting the standards of how tasks need to be done, and redoing them to these standards after our partner performed a task. It is a cognitive strategy, these experts say, a way of dealing with high performance expectations and all the fear of failure they induce.

After all, if our kids, our homes, our lives are "perfect," no one can ever find fault with us. We'll escape unscathed, unharmed, *unashamed*.

Gatekeeping doesn't just happen to moms: as the *Wall Street Journal* reported on a 2018 study published in Academy of Management, "Women in the workplace struggle to delegate tasks, are more likely to feel guilty about doing so and tend to have less-courteous interactions with subordinates when they do pass on tasks." Doing it all ourselves may pay off in the short run, but over time—as we just discussed—there are costs.

I knew I needed to find a different way forward. These days, when my husband cleans our hundred-year-old hardwood floors with Windex, feeds the kids pasta twice in one day, or dresses them in play clothes for a party, I let it slide. I physically restrain myself from remaking the bed after he's already done it. Because I know: my constantly correcting him does nothing to build his confidence or competence. Besides this, does it really matter if the bedsheets don't match the duvet and the pillows aren't perfectly fluffed? Is someone, really, going to judge me? And if they do . . . do I really care?

Whoever taught us that clean countertops were more important than our sanity doesn't have our best interests at heart. This message—that a woman needs to be all and do all, perfectly, in order to avoid social devaluation and protect her identity—is not a message I want to pass on to my kids. My daughter, Molly, is watching.

Brené Brown talks about "minding the gap" between our ideals and our lived experience, and making a commitment to practice the values that we *truly* consider important. ("We don't have to be perfect," Brown reminds us in *Daring Greatly*, "just engaged and committed to aligning values with action.") This is what I call on myself, and my partner, to do.

Thanks to shame resilience, I am learning that not everything—from the "success" of my marriage to the quality of every meal I prepare to the condition of our stroller—is a reflection of my self and my worth. But for the first three or so years of our marriage, my expectations were impossibly high—so much higher than Arran's—and I was determined to meet them, no matter the physical, mental, and emotional costs.

"My husband knows I need to work," Christa says. "He knows my work affords our life here and he values my work." Still, Christa finds herself taking on the bulk of the household labor, including the responsibilities associated with the kids, and resenting her husband for it.

"I think many men don't know what's involved and are happy to stay a bit ignorant and weaponize their incompetence and just sort of coast instead of doing the actual work to see what it takes to be actually involved," Christa says.

"And it's because it's deep down ingrained that it's the women's work. Even as we get some equality they think 'Sure, they should get paid the same and they can have high-powered jobs' but I don't think there has been a lot of work to defend care work. My husband legitimately thinks I 'just know' what to do when it comes to raising kids. He thinks I enjoy making the lunches and making sure they have clothes and that, because I'm a woman, I inherently know how to raise them (and not that I spent hours researching and thinking).

"On a surface level, him 'helping' with the kids is enough," she continues. "Many people would point to his parenting as super involved. And he is. But he and I are working out of different frameworks. That is our problem. He'll sometimes say, 'My dad never changed a diaper! I'm doing so much more!' So for him he's moved the needle, and he thinks that should be enough."

It's exhausting to have to deprogram ourselves and our partners. This is why men need to do the work. If we've partnered with people that truly share our values, then those partners need to educate themselves on everything—from potty training to the patriarchy—with the same ferocity that we do.

They, too, need to develop the critical awareness. And there are content creators who will hold their hands, so we don't have to. Relationship consultant Zach Watson shares videos chock-full of personal and universal examples of how couples fail at sharing the domestic, mental, and emotional load. He recommends books and highlights their practical strategies—like Eve Rodsky's *Fair Play* and its suggestion that couples have agreed upon minimum standards for household tasks.

Watson acknowledges, like Christa and so many of the women I interviewed, that men have good intentions, they want to help, but as he put it in a recent Instagram reel, "Going to your partner with anything that requires thought, calculation, and consideration of other things rather than options is load adding."

Watson is just one smart, accessible expert our partners can follow. And there are other resources. Read the books and follow the accounts, my dude!

Men need to do this work for the sake of the marriage—for our happiness, as well as theirs. A 2019 study of married couples found that women's sexual desire declined more steeply over time than did men's sexual desire, which did not decline on average, and that declines in women's but not men's sexual desire predicted declines in both partners' marital satisfaction. The causes of sexless marriage can be complicated and relate to health issues, trauma, childbirth, a lack of communication, and stress—it is also a factor that no one wants to fuck a dependent, and studies say that's what men who don't contribute equally become in their partner's mind. According to a 2022 study published in the *Archives of Sexual Behavior*, when women do more household labor, we see our partners as a dependent, and sexual desire dries right up.

Call on your partner to educate himself. And if he isn't willing to do this, I tell my friends (and I tell you now): you deserve more.

When I received Anne Helen Petersen's Substack newsletter titled "Blue Marriage and the Terror of Divorce," it struck a nerve. "In a culture that ostensibly celebrates strong, independent women," she asks, why does a fear of divorce remain? According to Petersen, it's about money and keeping things together "for the kids" and avoiding shame and loss of social capital.

Interestingly, though, while the fear of the "shame of divorce" often keeps women in a difficult relationship . . . my reporting shows that once they exit that relationship, many women leave shame behind without a second thought.

I was taken by Lyz Lenz's 2020 essay in *Glamour*: "It Took Divorce to Make My Marriage Equal." She spent twelve years fighting for an equal partnership, she writes, "when what I needed was divorce.

"I'd spent the past two years begging for help with the kids and housework, only to be told that I could just quit my job if it was all too much. 'It's not too much,' I'd said over and over. 'It's just not all my job.'" After accommodating his job, his career, Lenz says, "I realized it would never be my turn." Instead of endlessly bargaining for child-free hours, she sought a divorce and requested (and received) a custody agreement that mandated that the two of them bear equal childcare responsibility.

My divorced friend Lilli describes the end of her marriage as "the best thing that ever happened to me.

"Some of my friends are truly happy for me but they don't want to hear details. They're stuck in the box," Lilli says. "But being divorced is opening my mind more and more, and my friends are telling me the realities of their marriage.

"Divorced friends can smell a shit marriage from a mile away," Lilli continues, "but we can't say anything. No one can say, 'You should absolutely leave him.' That needs to come from inside them. And not everyone is ready or able to face the reality of divorce and living alone. All I can, and do, say to them is, 'It doesn't have to be this way.' And 'You deserve better. You deserve to be treated better. You deserve to be happy.' Those are things that took me years to realize. For years, it didn't even occur to me that divorce was a possibility. It's hard, but it's better. I had no idea how much better life could be."

It reminds me of this quote from Allison Robicelli's piece on the website *Gloria*, "When I tell men about my divorce, they agree it is sad. They all say they're so sorry. They know it's a tragedy. They never say congratulations. Their wives do, though."

Embracing the Suck

"Pandemic living flattened my life and my identity," Angela Garbes writes in her book *Essential Labor: Mothering as Social Change*.

I could no longer be the same person out in the world. I began to doubt my own sense of self. For months I secretly wished that my creative impulse, the urge to write, would just die. Then, I thought, I would at least be free of the guilt and shame of wanting more, of being unable to find fulfillment in caring for my family.

Oh, if I had read these words back then—during the pandemic, but even before then, when I, too, was "sheltering in place"—how I would have related. As it was, I felt very alone.

For the first six months of the pandemic, the 2016 Disney film *Moana* played on repeat. I would put it on in the morning to distract—excuse me, *engage*—my toddlers, but I found that it inspired me as I waded through the slog. Folding pile after endless pile of laundry, I, too, felt as if I had been staring at the edge of the water as long as I could remember, never really knowing why. When my husband and I bickered about who overfilled the garbage bin, when I flinched with jealousy at a friend online announcing her professional success, when I sobbed with guilt and frustration after raging at the dog, I heard Moana whisper, *This is not who you are.*

Moana, we are told, is different from the skinny white princesses of Disney past. Her thick calves and brown skin differentiate her. There is no love interest in Moana. The heroine was chosen by the spirit of the ocean to save her people. She is told by her father that she must stay on the island. No one leaves the island. But the ocean calls.

I am Moana. The ocean calls. On Twitter, an editor posts a call for pitches. I have an idea I want to send off, but without childcare, writing is impossible, so instead of realizing my potential I have to be a half-ass mom, bitter and resentful at playing with a tea set or picking up the markers for the five hundredth time instead of using my advanced degrees and god-given talents to contribute to society and engage with public life. I log off Twitter and log onto Instagram and get sucked into a string of reels featuring twentysomething-year-old stay-at-home moms talking about keto diets. I pick up last night's ice cream dishes and consider squeezing in a spin class while my then one-year-old daughter stares at the screen.

I am Moana. Strong-willed, defiant. A natural way-finder, using all my talents and advanced degrees to find my way to the kitchen, where dishes pile up in the sink. In my head I cuss out my husband for forgetting to turn on the dishwasher. I add detergent, hit start, pull up the Target order online, and add Cascade Complete.

I am also Moana's mother. Every morning that I wake up without childcare, I turn to myself, just as in one scene Moana turns to her mother, and I tell myself: *Sometimes, who we wish we were, and what we wish we could do, it's just not meant to be.*

I am the lava monster, too, obviously. Who is also—spoiler alert—the goddess Te Fiti. Like, I am a total goddess. I'm just really fucking pissed.

I didn't know about perinatal anxiety and depression. I hadn't yet heard the phrase "touched out." I didn't know in an intellectual way how the constant invasion of a mother's personal space can lead to anxiety, irritability, and revulsion, followed closely by guilt. And for survivors of sexual violence in particular, even normal bids for attention can feel overly demanding.

I only know that I had had enough. At two and three and sometimes four in the morning, while the newborn slept, I rocked our firstborn even as my own body begged for sleep. Even as my own circuitry yearned to be soothed, I prioritized the needs of my son and, to a lesser extent, my husband. Until I couldn't do it anymore. My body hit a wall and I was done.

I did not know about caregiver burnout and that parents and mothers especially—and especially the mothers of special-needs children—need support so that they can support their kids. I thought it was my job as "mom."

An expert I'd interviewed for an article once advised me to see myself and my husband as a team, but I could not—as she put it then—"embrace the suck." I did not see us as a team. I saw no way out and at times I wanted to die because I saw no other solution to the tremendous amount of stress accumulating in my body. Solutions like basic income and collective child-rearing felt pie in the sky.

I blamed myself. And I blamed my husband, Arran.

I felt, as Garbes puts it, "the white-hot frustration—overdependency on my spouse, the thought that maybe my work really isn't as valuable as his—felt so personal. It was hard not to think there was a flaw in me, that I had made nothing but wrong choices."

Who had time for closing the gender pay gap by acknowledging how care work and career interruptions impact a woman's lifetime earning potential? I was physically, mentally, and emotionally exhausted. I was demoralized, and just trying to survive.

That's when it hit me: all this shame, and its effect on us, isn't by accident—it's by design.

"Each day I fight to remind myself that these are not personal or lifestyle problems," Garbes continues, "and they are not even pandemic-specific: these are systemic issues that have been built into labor and financial institutions; they are, by design, foundational to American life."

Learning to Live Differently

In the spirit of shame resilience, I talk about my feelings, and shame, with other cisgender women, transgender individuals, and nonbinary folks because we are the ones most harmed by sexist shame and gender oppression. But it's important, and illuminating, to do this work with cisgender men, too.

"As a straight white male in the US, I am expected to be a lot of things," Al tells me. "A provider, a protector, a man, a patriot, successful, happy, and secure in my identity." Men, too, fall into the trap of compare and despair: "Who's tougher? Who makes more money? Who's in better physical shape? Don't be weak or emotional (like a bitch)."

Listening to him now, it's hard to imagine that this is the same knucklehead I went to high school with.

"I grew up desperately wanting friends and to be popular," he admits. "I thought that being the wild kid or the IDGAF kid was respected and cool, when in fact it made me the butt of a joke most times. As I got older I realized that I wanted to be seen and heard. I wanted friends that respected and cared about me specifically and not just the party I could get them into or the crazy things I was willing to do for a laugh.

"As hard as we try to let men be emotional or openly loving or caring, there are equal forces pushing for us to still be a stereotypical masculine figure," Al continues. "I don't see that changing. If anything, nowadays, you're expected to be both masculine and a 'modern' man."

Ricky was a star athlete in high school. "You subconsciously drape yourself in that," he tells me now. "I'm smart and educated, but [the athlete identity]—that's where I got my biscuits. As a Black man, especially, I was told it'd be my way out."

But after high school, Ricky says a career in football didn't materialize, so he went into coaching. "My wife would look at me and say, 'You tell me you like coaching, but you look miserable. You come home and look drained.' When I sat back and thought about it, I was very uneasy. I thought, 'Is this it?' I was doing what I was supposed to. I couldn't be Ricky the athlete anymore so I became Ricky the coach. It was safe, but it wasn't me. It was what everyone else thought.

"Shame made me feel less than," Ricky says. Underneath the accolades, he says, "I felt emotionally inadequate.

"Shame fueled my dishonesty with my loved ones and myself. I lied so that I could get back to a place of emotional security. In most situations, the shame was fueled by my own self-talk or negative conversations with myself. If I was only honest from the start, my loved ones were a lot more understanding and sympathetic to my situation."

Then the pandemic, and the murder of George Floyd, happened. Ricky describes it as a time of tiredness. "I stopped coaching," he says. "And I stopped caring what people thought. Quarantine time, we surrendered. It was much needed, and we wanted to. It quieted our household. It slowed us down completely."

Ricky was hospitalized for COVID and lost two friends to the disease. "It was like, Screw this," he said. "I told myself, I'm not going back."

"I felt bad about abandoning the kids I coached, but it was what I wanted to do and what my family needed," he says. "Before then, I was doing things for my family through the lens of what everyone else thought my family needed."

Today, Ricky is a stay-at-home dad. "I do the cooking, the cleaning, all of it. The roles are reversed. I know society expects me to be alpha male, head of household, Andrew Tate—just very stereotypical male. But I understand my purpose, and I'm very comfortable with my role in my family.

"My role in my family is to make sure they have what they need," Ricky says. "My children need me. My wife needs me to be there for my children. This is what she wants. My wife is a partner at a law firm—she's always made more money. It is her preference. And honestly, I'm probably more of the person who should be with the kids every day, I'm more nurturing, I'm more the feelings person, whereas my wife is more analytical."

To flip the roles in this way, "it takes working through a lot of hang-ups.

"Shame breaking comes from communication," Ricky says. Whatever the shame, "if you're not talking about it, you're in trouble. My wife and I have gotten to a good place and rediscovered each other from recalibrating and having the talk. Now I'm more in tune to myself. When I might be feeling a certain way," he says, "I ask myself, Where is that feeling coming from? As a parent, I talk about my feelings more with my kids. I explain why I'm reacting a certain way or not. I teach them about shame. I tell them it's a pressure, and it's relentless. Shame will tell you that life needs to look a kind of way. But it doesn't. It doesn't have to be that way."

Wholeheartedness means giving both yourself as well as those you love permission to be vulnerable and to live in the truth. Now, any time I feel myself pulling back instead of opening up, or closing down rather than allowing myself to fully experience whatever it is I am encountering, I soften to the emotional experience, without hesitation, without rejecting or retreating into myself. I listen to what my body is trying to say. It is the same body that has carried me all along.

Learning to better understand our difficult feelings, and dedicating time for meaningful conversations about them, has become a saving grace for our marriage. Arran and I are less reactive with each other. Any slights or major disagreements are mostly saved for a weekly family meeting. These one- or two-hour conversations—held when the children aren't around and my husband and I are both relaxed and less emotional—give us an opportunity to reflect on why we are feeling crummy and to troubleshoot the week ahead.

It's all part of a concerted effort to do things differently, an effort we've both committed to make. To cultivate gladness, we remind each other to stay in the present. It's hard for us intellectual types, but happiness takes getting out of our heads, noticing and savoring the sensual experience of the moment before us. In this moment, nothing is missing. Nothing is wrong. There are no *if onlys*. No *If only I were different*. No *If only I could get more done*. This moment is enough. I am enough. I am adequate. So is he.

At a family meeting, we discuss and divide work, including each task's mental load. We negotiate and agree on minimum standards. When I swallowed my pride and admitted that I needed help, my husband started coming up with solutions. We started hiring childcare when we could, even though it didn't make financial sense (in the long run, it did).

I also started to make myself completely unavailable, physically, mentally, and emotionally, for hours and sometimes days at a time.

In her book *Forget "Having It All": How America Messed Up Motherhood—and How to Fix It*, journalist Amy Westervelt suggests a "strategic absence" as a way of lessening those demands and equalizing the invisible load that often falls on mothers. As I reported in a 2020 article for *Elemental*, titled "Short-Term Abandonment of

Your Loved Ones May Help Your Mental Health," the term is typically applied in the world of business and refers to the practice of
those in leadership positions taking time off and making themselves
unavailable as a way of testing and increasing the capacity of the rest
of their staff. It's also used in the political context to describe the
belief that, in foreign affairs, it is sometimes better to be absent than
involved.

In this context, the term comes from the work of researcher and
motherhood expert Petra Bueskens and refers to periods of time
when Mom's not around. According to Bueskens in her book *Modern Motherhood and Dual Identities*, periodic maternal absences can
generate a "structural and psychological shift in the family," disrupt-
ing the default position typically assigned to mothers and requiring
fathers or other caretakers to take on a much more active role.

Strategic absence is not just for married women with children. If
you find yourself taking on a particular dynamic with the people
you live with—if you're the roommate who always cleans the kitchen,
for example, or the adult sibling shouldering the responsibility of
attending to your aging parent's needs—strategic absence might
help you, too.

The point of strategic absence is that it puts the labor your partner
discounts front and center. If either you or your partner feels you
couldn't function without the other, strategic absence disabuses a
family of this belief. It reveals to everyone that there are different
ways of doing things. And yes, it alleviates feelings of burnout and
improves mental health.

Arran and I started slowly. For three hours at a time I would go to
a coffee shop with my computer, a journal, or a book and I would

work, or write, or read. Or not. How I used the time away was less important than the fact that I was getting it.

When my kids were both school-aged, and with my husband's encouragement, I started renting a camper van in the woodsy suburbs for weeks at a time where I can go and work. It's not as romantic as it sounds. I'm not talking about some honey-colored nomadic fantasy you'd see if you search the hashtag "vanlife." We're talking about a big white van parked in someone's driveway. It's not exactly remote. And far from luxurious—there's no running water. No hot shower. No toilet. I don't care. Are my kids there? No? Fantastic; I poop on puppy training pads.

I use my time away to work, but I'm also connecting to myself— a woman, it turns out, that I actually like. And sure, when I come home from a weekend in the van, the house is trashed. The garbage is overflowing. The inch of milk left in the carton is spoiled. The kids have built a "bad guy trap" cascading down the staircase. My husband has hung fairy lights in the kids' bedroom, even though I've made it clear to him that I think fairy lights are gauche.

I bite my tongue. I ask myself, Does it really matter? It's their house, too. So what if it isn't up to my aesthetic standards. Everyone is safe. They're having fun.

They're happy.

For the most part, I'm happy, too.

8

Hoes Before Literally Everything

Making Friendship Matter

In October 2020, the *Atlantic* asked readers to consider how it might be different if friendship, not marriage, was at the center of life. The article highlighted a handful of individuals with friends who played a role in each other's lives that is typically reserved for romantic partners. I'm talking about deep and complex relationships including women who put each other, rather than their husbands, first. While the article addressed the fact that there is no word for these kinds of intimate friendships, when my mom friends and I passed it around in our group over text, we had a playful suggestion: sister wives.

During the height of the pandemic, this is what we called each other. When daycares shuttered and husbands everywhere closed the doors of their home offices, leaving their wives to deal with—*gestures wildly at everything*—we became each other's one and only sources of support.

The love I feel for women keeps me alive. It nurtures compassion and reacquaints me with the love I feel for myself. Yes, female friendship is fraught—but we can't do it alone. We can't overly rely on our romantic partners either. Instead, platonic love is where it's at, or so I'm learning.

Best Friends Come with Benefits

"I'd been married for about five minutes before I realized this man would never/will never be enough to 'complete me,' aka fulfill my emotional needs," says poet Kate Baer in a conversation with author Sara Petersen on her *In Pursuit of Clean Countertops* newsletter. "The pressure that puts on him! And me! And us!" She goes on to "wonder if some of the happiest marriages are not two people but a whole crew of humans who can fill the gaps." Her husband, she says, "is great, but he has no idea what it feels like to have a postpartum perineum, a vested interest in Mindy Kaling's career journey, or the unbridled need to dance to Megan Thee Stallion. Yes, I talk to him about my deepest, darkest fears," Baer says. "but then I rehash it 7,000 times with my circle of women until they can repeat it for themselves. I do the same for them."

We all need this. We all need friends who we trust will have our backs, safe containers that can hold our most uncomfortable truths. Someone to text, literally in the middle of a fight with our significant other, for a temperature check. People who, when you ask *Am I the asshole*, will sometimes answer, kindly, yes. People who really know us, who we respect, and who respect us enough to hold us accountable to our truths.

Let it be said that I find the typical way of getting to know people extremely uncomfortable. You can save the small talk. I don't want to talk about our hobbies. I want to talk about our obsessions. I want to hear your unfiltered fears. Don't tell me about your trip to Costco this past weekend. Tell me about the last time you cried. Let's get our shame out there on the table and pick over its carcass, together.

Psychologists might accuse me of trauma bonding. Brené Brown talks about how oversharing is actually a shame shield, and the opposite of vulnerability. So is being the cool kid that finds making friends "boring." I don't entirely disagree.

I'm learning to take friendships more slowly, and to maybe not lead with the most shocking and presumably shameful things about me. Instead of starting a conversation with "Do you like to poop? I LOVE to poop! Ever get a hemorrhoid? I used to be a hooker. One time I bit my kid. How much money do you make? I have seasonal depression! Do you watch *90 Day Fiancé*?" I am learning to pause. Slow down and trust. I am learning to love listening as much as I love talking. I am learning the art of gently leaning into points of connection, including our vulnerabilities. By taking it slow, Brown says we increase the chance of it becoming what she calls a "Big Friendship," which she defines in part as "a bond of great strength, force, and significance that transcends life phases, geography, and emotional shifts."

Thanks to the conversations I had in writing this book, I believe even more strongly that allyship, platonic love, and female friendships can free us from shame and usher us toward happier, more fulfilling lives. Nothing could replace the connection I feel toward other women.

Friendships do more than contribute to our happiness. Research suggests they literally keep us alive. In *Monitor on Psychology*, Zara Abrams reports, "Psychological research suggests that stable, healthy friendships are crucial for our well-being and longevity. . . . People who have friends and close confidantes are more satisfied with their lives and less likely to suffer from depression. They're also less likely to die from all causes, including heart problems and a range of chronic diseases."

Research finds that friendships between women are particularly beneficial to our health. Clinical psychologist and author Molly Millwood describes this as "The Female Effect," which is "when two (or more) women who know and trust each other simply spend time together, they experience increases in oxytocin, which in turn increase feelings of empathy and fondness for one another and decrease cortisol, which is the stress hormone."

For women, camaraderie is also good for our careers: a 2019 study of recent MBA grads, for example, found that women who have a strong circle of friends are more likely to get executive positions with high pay.

We all need, if not an entire table of besties to be there at our birthday dinner, at least one or more women we can count on to hold our hand through hard times, or to put in a good word with the boss. As the saying goes: men will grab your ass, but women will save it. Of course, it's not as simple as that. I spoke to women who admitted struggling to connect with other women. ("I never relate well to groups of women," "I feel awkward around other females," and "I can't be myself" were common refrains.)

"I was horribly bullied and never learned to make friends in elementary school," Amy admits. "It turns out I'm neurodivergent so it's not such a surprise. I still am not great at connecting deeply."

Morgan says she grew up watching *Sex and the City* "without realizing how empowering or liberating that show was. Sadly, I learned that *Sex and the City* is television and not reality. Women still are not allowed to have honest, candid conversations about sex."

Morgan admits that she's part of the problem: "There was an instance, once, in which a female shared with me her sexual experience with a guy. She said he became oddly aggressive in their encounter and that it had left her feeling shook afterward.

"I gaslit her experience," Morgan admits. "I said that I couldn't see that guy behaving in that way. I feel so ashamed of this now," Morgan continues, "but I actually shared her experience with a couple girlfriends, passing judgment on her. As karma would have it, I later found myself on the receiving end in a similar situation. It took going through something similar to see how hurtful my actions were."

We've all been on both sides of situations like this. We are all familiar with gossip, competition, and other by-products of shame. These habits are ingrained in all of us. They threaten relationships between women and undermine our power and inhibit our joy.

Author Kelly Valen surveyed three-thousand-plus women for her 2010 book *The Twisted Sisterhood* and found that almost 90 percent frequently felt "currents of meanness and negativity emanating from other females."

Perhaps you can relate?

Make Friends (and Keep Them!) by Practicing Empathy

Empathy is defined simply as the ability to understand and share the feelings of another. It means putting ourselves in another person's shoes, and seeing the world through their perspective. Empathy has no script, writes Brené Brown in *Daring Greatly*. "There is no right way or wrong way to do it. It's simply listening, holding space, without judgment, emotionally connecting, and communicating that incredibly healing message of 'You are not alone.'"

We've all been there: a friend is sobbing because her dirtbag boyfriend cheated on her (again!). Sure, he's a creep, but in your eyes, she's handling the situation poorly. Instead of being supportive, you're brutally judging her.

Part of the reason we may lack empathy, as a 2005 study by Loren Toussaint and John R. Webb observed, is that women more than men are trained to compare each other from an early age. We hold other women to the same harsh standards that we hold for ourselves. Sometimes the more we recognize our sameness, the more we are likely to feel intolerance or contempt. Similarly, the jealousy we feel toward other women is frequently tied to our own inner critic, a harsh voice in our own head that whispers we are not enough and shames us into bad behavior.

If this is your experience, awareness is the first step. In her advice column called *The Business of Friendship*, Shasta Nelson recommends we recognize difficult feelings directed toward other women "as an opportunity to get curious about yourself."

As Nelson writes, "Envy isn't something to be ashamed about." Instead of rushing to dismiss mean or unwarranted thoughts, she says, investigate them. "Hard feelings toward others present an opportunity to gather information about your own deep-seated needs and desires."

After this kind of inquiry, bring compassion to yourself. Then extend that loving-kindness toward another. Use the information you gather to guide your actions in a way that aligns with your ideals.

In a recent newsletter, friendship expert and author Anna Goldfarb asked the age-old question: How can friendships survive the arrival of children? "It's not enough to imagine how your friends are feeling," Goldfarb contends. Instead, "Imagine what [your] parent friend *needs* at this moment in their life."

Anna continues, "Unless they have around-the-clock help, most parents are focused chiefly on survival when kiddos are young. Things like sleeping, eating, and paying bills. I get it; fun takes a back seat when you're trying to keep a tiny human alive. My strategy, as a nonparent, is to help my parent friend meet their most immediate needs."

Anna goes on to describe the time one friend was chronically exhausted after she'd had her second child. "I stopped trying to organize happy hours and fancy lunch dates together. Instead, I came over to her house every week to watch her kiddos so she could take a nap."

Empathetic relationships start with an acknowledgment that our feelings are real. Even the resentment we feel toward each other is real, however misdirected. For example, reporting in the *Economist* in 2023 states that fat women have lower starting wages and lower lifetime earning potential than women who are not fat. And this is just true for women, mind you—not men. Thin women, in other words, have a wage premium. It is no wonder we feel pressure to be thin—and, possibly, in competition with our thinner coworkers. Even though people are rarely in control of their weight, we accurately perceive that failing to lose or maintain a certain weight will literally cost us.

Thin privilege is real, and it is reasonable for us to call on one another to dismantle it.

Pretty privilege is real, too. After Janet Mock began to medically transition at fifteen, she writes for *Allure*, "how I saw myself inside began to slowly and steadily reveal itself on my outsides.

"I did nothing to earn the attention my prettiness granted me," writes Mock. "I soon saw that people stared and smiled, offered me seats on the bus and drinks in the club, complimented me on my appearance, and held doors open.

"Being able to blend in is a gateway to survival," Mock writes, "but many trans women do not benefit from my passing privilege or my pretty privilege."

On Facebook, Mock underscored her argument: "People with privilege do not want to discuss their privilege—whether it's privilege derived from whiteness, straightness, cisness. But we must acknowledge our privilege if we are to dismantle these systems and hierarchies."

We all have our "pain points"—that is, the parts of ourselves that we are ashamed about. We all compare ourselves to other women, even as this behavior separates and segregates us from others rather than drawing us closer.

Sara says her pain point is "an inability to be neat and tidy in my office and home. It seems to be this expected part of femininity that I am missing. I try to stop myself from doing it because I know it isn't helpful, but it's impossible not to compare." Sara adds, "I definitely compare my looks, too. Particularly skin. At the moment I am noticing age-related changes. All the comparing comes with 'shoulds' and it always feels shitty."

"I have diastasis recti and compare my midsection to other moms in real life," Shabana admits. "When I was on social media, I noticed things I didn't care about before, like the lines on my neck."

"I'm really great at finding someone better than me at whatever I'm doing, and I'm not happy until I reach that level of success," Karie says. "There is always someone doing it better, so it never fucking ends." In Karie's case, she says, "I never resent the person. My frustration or anger is always directed at myself."

For some of us, as we grow older, it's even painfully more obvious how we can't compete—with other women, with the fictional ideal, even with our past selves.

Some women I spoke to—like sixty-six-year-old Lisa—had come to terms with the way aging changed them, and were happily entering a new phase in life. "As far as looks, body image, etc.—well, that ship has sailed! If it's between me and a younger woman, I'd lose. I'm just not 'in the running' anymore. That feels fine."

Penny shares this sentiment. "Appearance and body image used to be something I would self-punish for but as I get older, I feel less stress around it and more self-acceptance."

But other women I spoke to hadn't reached this place yet. "As I age, and skin starts to sag, my body looks even more gross to me, more wrong," my one friend shares. "I see other women at the pool, in the shower—and how they've aged, or how young they are—and I feel envious and ashamed."

It all begins with acknowledging uncomfortable truths. If not, shame proliferates between us and the people we could potentially love, including the person in the mirror. For a long time, I blamed my status as a former sex worker as the thing that kept me from connecting. But let's be real, even before working in the sex industry—and even before moving to the suburbs and navigating friendships as a woman with a provocative past (which, I've come to realize, is all of us)—I harbored fears, suspicions, anger, and other hard feelings toward other women. To be sure, I'm not the only woman out there with a concealable stigmatized identity. We all have good reasons to be guarded. But we can move past that fear—and we must.

Becoming a Good Neighbor

When Oscar was around sixteen months old, I found myself desperate for human contact. By then I had naturally moved away from the recovery community, and had lost contact with a lot of the girl-friends I'd met in the rooms of AA. Arran and I had left the city and were living in the suburbs, and had yet to bridge the fenced-in lawns and fear of dissimilarity that divided us from our neighbors. Sure, I had found online communities, but I hungered for more than a good deal on Facebook Marketplace.

In search of daily witnesses, I began to put my body in the periphery of other women with children. That's how I met Natalie, in the children's section of the public library. During open playtime, she and I were engaging in our own version of parallel play when one of us dared break the ice. I forget how the conversation came up, but at some point I dared to profess that stay-at-home mothering wasn't what I thought it'd be.

"Oh yeah, I thought I'd be home canning jam, yeah right, that happened," Natalie said with a laugh.

That was it. I had found a bitch I liked.

I'll never knock digital friendships, but I readily admit that virtual connections can't perfectly replace the benefits of connection that happen In Real Life. A long-distance relative can offer advice and commiseration, but they can't help you look for your missing cat or leave a children's fever reducer on the porch when the whole family is sick. They can't look into your eyes or give you a hug. This sort of comfort can only come from the people in close proximity.

Natalie introduced me to other moms who, in no time, became like family to me. These women showed up for me in tangible, practical ways—offering playdates, swapping hand-me-downs, exchanging resources—all of which cultivated a feeling of belonging in a new and unfamiliar place. They made my life less painful and shameful. At the time, the fact that my newly suburban husband and I didn't have a car was a source of ongoing stress and real shame. No matter, my new pal Laura said, she would drive Oscar to daycare. She sat with me when Oscar was sick and Arran was at work.

Shortly after Molly was born, Laura organized the meal train. Night after night, our neighbors sustained us: vegan risotto rich with roasted butternut squash and sage served with a lemony kale salad studded with dried cranberries and pistachios; roasted eggplant and tomato orzo with a side of butter lettuce drenched in mustardy vinaigrette; mujadara—a signature Middle Eastern dish of lentils and rice garnished with crispy onions; mushroom barley soup, thick and piping hot; loaves and loaves of crusty sourdough bread, all home cooked and delivered with care.

These meals, and the company, sustained us. And returning the favors reminded us of our basic goodness.

"On some level, we all crave connection. We want to live with a sense of being known and knowing the people closest to us. We want to be part of a community," journalist Peter Lovenheim, author of *In the Neighborhood: The Search for Community on an American Street, One Sleepover at a Time*, told me for an article on the subject of neighboring for *Real Simple*.

"Knowing your neighbors affects everything from the crime rate to life expectancy," Dave Runyon, coauthor of *The Art of Neighboring*, told me for the same piece. Runyon is executive director of CityUnite, a nonprofit that helps faith, government, and business leaders work together, as well as a former pastor. He said that because we don't choose neighbors the same way we choose friends, "you are guaranteed to be in relationships with people who think about the world differently than you do. If polarization is dividing our culture, relationships with our neighbors are the antidote."

Loving your neighbors, says Runyon, starts with one gesture: learn, remember, and use their names. "This can be super awkward," he concedes, particularly if you've lived somewhere for years or they've introduced themselves to you multiple times.

Runyon's motto: "Lean in to awkward."

While shame is an impediment to friendship, losing our shame paves the way to closer relationships. As sensitivities about our own perceived inadequacies soften, the more we see strangers as friends.

Solidarity Saves Lives

We are responsible for one another's well-being. We can be responsible for the harm or the healing. These are everyday choices we make. Who we invite, or not, to our backyard barbecue, who we include or exclude from the group chat, who we invite or leave out when the coworkers all go out for lunch. It's natural to have biases. Just remember: who we turn toward and away from informs which parts of ourselves we accept and reject. The term "respectability politics" was coined in 1993 by historian Evelyn Brooks Higginbotham and is generally understood to describe the political strategy that members of a marginalized community may consciously or unconsciously adopt in order to fit in.

"Respectability politics are rooted in resistance to racist imagery of Black people, particularly Black women, who adopted self-presentation strategies that downplayed sexuality and emphasized morality and dignity to reject White America's stereotypes of them," writes Mikaela Pitcan, Alice Marwick, and danah boyd in their essay, "Performing a Vanilla Self: Respectability Politics, Social Class, and the Digital World," published in the May 2018 issue of *Journal of Computer-Mediated Communication.*

By downplaying or punishing others for displaying aspects of a cultural-political identity, certain members of a marginalized group are able to assimilate and achieve social mobility. But the politics of respectability, these researchers say, "ignores structural inequalities that remain unchallenged and unchanged" and "reinforces within-group stratification to juxtapose a respectable us against a shameful other."

The biggest threat to female friendship and empowerment, as I see it, is prejudice—that is, a fear of difference. From clique-y friend groups to powerful feminist institutions purportedly fighting for all women's rights, white women have long excluded folks who don't abide by the mainstream standards of appearance or behavior that we ourselves have consciously or unconsciously sought to uphold. More and more, "diverse" folks are being offered a seat at the table. But what parts of them, and ourselves, are we still unwilling or unable to acknowledge?

The cost of this exclusion is too great. In *Weathering: The Extraordinary Stress of Ordinary Life in an Unjust Society,* Arline T. Geronimus documents how social structures create worse health outcomes for marginalized folks. She uses the term "weathering" to describe how aging is affected by literal environmental exposures, by material hardship, and by your biopsychosocial exposures.

As Geronimus explains in an interview on the website *Gloria,* when marginalized folks are exposed to inhospitable environments, "environments that are not made for you historically, or where there are not many people like you, that itself is weathering," adding that "that's the kind of exposure that more higher-income people of color or other marginalized groups are exposed to, more than low-income people, or even the most impoverished."

For *Business Insider,* I spoke to Lydia Elle, a diversity coach who runs workshops and mentors staff at all levels. Elle says that when it comes to questions like race, gender, sexuality, and other individual differences, people are overwhelmed and afraid of saying or doing the wrong thing.

"The first and most vital step towards these fixing issues is being aware and acknowledging them. We cannot move to a place of healing and growth without speaking first about what is sick."

We are less likely to make a mistake if we start from the assumption that all bodies deserve dignity and respect. This, as I understand it, is the opposite of the way shame operates in our society. We must start with a deep and profound respect for the impact that shame has on people's lives, and acknowledge that people with multiple marginalized identities experience shame and shaming disproportionately. This is a powerful reframe.

I think back to all those years I struggled to fit in. The years I concealed my status as a sex worker. The years following that, when I tried to differentiate myself from other sex workers, leaning awkwardly on my education and the fact that I didn't do drugs to differentiate myself from "what some people might think." Obeying shame was a losing strategy. Eventually, I realized that my desire to feel and appear normal could no longer come at the expense of others, and that no one's respectability should rely on another's disrepute. All those years, I fought for the right to believe that I was fit, in spite of all my mistakes, and to believe I'd done my best, even when it was my worst. For years, I fought to feel normal, just like everyone else. But to be human, according to James Baldwin, is not something one must fight for: "We need only to do what is infinitely more difficult— that is, accept it."

I am aware that when white women speak for and as the authoritative, universal voice, we ignore how race functions to inform some aspects of sexism. White women like myself can be willfully ignorant to how racism privileges us over women of color, Black women in particular, and how our ignorance contributes to their oppression.

I've taken actions to educate myself, but I still fuck up all the time. In this book, I've probably taken my positionality for granted countless times. I make no declaration to perfection—only a commitment to this process, which extends beyond my lifetime. A process of taking responsibility. No, I'm not perfect. I am thinking and rethinking about the choices I make.

And I will never not be honest about the privileges I have, or not.

In chapter 1, I explained the difference between guilt and shame. Guilt is the not-great feeling you get when you've done something wrong, whereas shame is a global feeling of wrongness; it is less about what you've done as it is an indictment of who you are. In the podcast *On Shame and Accountability*, Brené Brown does a great job of unpacking what we commonly refer to as "white guilt." We don't normally think of guilt, and white guilt in particular, as productive, she says, but it's shame—not guilt—that shuts us down or pushes us to save face. If, right about now or at anytime, you're feeling shame over your role in the harming of someone else, ask yourself honestly, what more can you do?

We all need to do better, myself included—and we can. By redirecting our shame into productive guilt, and allowing that guilt to motivate us into better aligning our actions with our values, we can create a more equitable society in which all members feel physically and psychologically safe and secure.

Owning ourselves means showing our mess, and not denying

anything. Not abandoning any parts of ourselves that may not fit a certain image. This kind of wholeheartedness is an effort, these relationships take work. They are an investment, but as a consequence of that work, I have cultivated a community—friends, colleagues, and mentors who can be honest with one another, relationships where we can be messy and make mistakes, and no one is going to judge us and nothing is going to be taken away.

In *The Body Is Not an Apology*, Sonya Renee Taylor spells out what she calls the "unapologetic agreements." Radical self-love, she says, comes from being a good friend. It comes from engaging in a "curiosity-driven dialogue" rather than arguments and debate, and remembering that personal attacks, name-calling, heavy sarcasm, and general unkindness is unhelpful. It means a commitment to interrupting attempts to derail and assuming the best. Self-compassion starts with having compassion for and honoring other people's varied journeys, and celebrating difference. It requires an ability to repair things when you've made a mistake and acknowledging intent while addressing impact. We don't have to be a "bad person" to cause harm; we don't have to intend harm to have caused it. But it's not too late to make it right.

It's hard work, but if you do it, you have the connection you desire. I may not be rich, but I have something priceless that most if not all people want: a constellation of people that I can be honest with. I am so grateful for these people and the things they help me see, because they are honest and their honesty allows me to be honest, and to recognize my truths. I am proof that it is possible to cultivate new communities and environments that allow us to be seen and heard for who we are and not just who someone needs us to be, spaces where it no longer feels necessary to value what others think over how you feel, among people who give us the strength to continue speaking our truths.

These individual and communal acts of honesty and non-judgment are an act of resistance to our larger culture of shame.

Okay, but what happens when you do mess up?

In the book *Sorry, Sorry, Sorry: The Case for Good Apologies*, coauthors Marjorie Ingall and Susan McCarthy break down what to do when we have done wrong, in six and a half steps, summarized here by Allie Volpe for *Vox*:

1. Say you're sorry or that you apologize. Actually use the words "I'm sorry" or "I apologize."
2. Name or specify the infraction you're apologizing for.
3. Show that you understand why your actions were harmful and hurtful, and that you understand the effect your actions had on the other person.
4. Don't make excuses, but do offer an explanation if needed.
5. Say what you will do to ensure this situation won't happen again.
6. Offer to fix what's broken—whether that's buying your aunt a new lamp to replace the one you knocked off a table at Thanksgiving or offering to spend more time with a friend who feels neglected.

The half step, Volpe says, is to listen to the person you've wronged. Center their experiences and emotions, not yours.

Bad apologies, these experts say, minimize or evade responsibility, so avoid words like "obviously," "regrettable," or "unfortunate." Don't shift or confer blame. If you feel you are also owed an apology, save that for a separate conversation.

When you apologize, be prepared for a deeper conversation. Do it face-to-face and make it individual, as opposed to a mass apology over social media.

Finally, don't apologize when you aren't wrong. Women are maligned for apologizing too frequently and there may be some truth to that: we apologize out of shame. "I'm sorry" slips out as a way to diffuse tension, express regret, to say thanks. We apologize for our failures and for our success.

Women "rush to apologize at the slightest bit of trouble," observed Zoe Fenson in a piece for *The Week*. As an example, she cites Naomi Osaka who defeated Serena Williams in the 2018 US Open. Instead of beaming, she offered her opponent a tearful apology.

Focus on what you did, if anything. Never apologize for who you are.

In It Together, Even When We're Apart

As I began to open up and talk honestly with other mothers about presumably shameful topics, something miraculous happened: I realized that what I'd been through and what I was going through was normal. I wasn't the only person to have gone through it. Even if I couldn't relate to the exact details, I could relate to the feelings. It was normal, also, to simultaneously experience conflicting feelings and thoughts, or to not always feel the way I was "supposed" to feel.

To this day I surround myself with women who get it. Moms with kids like mine. Other freelancers hustling the same hustle. I spend hours in conversation with other women who remind me what I know all the way to my bones—I am an amazing parent, a successful professional, and an overall decent human being.

In the company of my female friends, I feel protected. I feel reassured, emboldened, and secure. Friends ease each other's suffering—but even better, we get the benefit of sharing in each other's success.

Meditation teacher Kimberly Brown, from Meditation with Heart, shared a quote in a recent newsletter that is often attributed to the Dalai Lama: "If I am happy only for myself, many fewer chances for happiness. If I am happy when good things happen to other people, billions more chances to be happy."

Brown offers the word "Muditā," a Pali and Sanskrit word that means delighting in others' happiness or success. "Muditā is the gladness that arises at a wedding, when someone you know gets a promotion, when you learn a country has an abundant harvest or a new baby is born," Brown explains. This joy—which we can cultivate at any time and no matter what we're personally going through—"dispels the boredom and cynicism," Brown says, and is "an escape from the blah."

I was just beginning to cultivate a little Muditā in my life, and so I was dismayed when schools reopened for in-person learning after the pandemic, we enrolled Oscar at our local public preschool, and things began to go awry. Almost immediately, he exhibited behaviors that his teacher and the administration described as concerning. After a lengthy evaluation process, Oscar was diagnosed with a handful of conditions and developmental delays. Eventually, those diagnoses led to him being asked to leave the school. It was a challenging, upsetting, and, yes, *shameful* time.

To be clear: I rarely feel ashamed of my son. Instead, I feel his struggles are somehow my fault. I wasn't enough to prevent this from happening; I should've or could've done something differently. This shame is reinforced by a society that doesn't understand his disability, a public school system that doesn't meet their federal obligations, and my own struggles to find and secure the help he needs.

My experience with a special-needs child was not just shameful, it was isolating. My son and his behaviors weren't always welcome among his peers, and that led to loneliness and further shame. Eventually, we were compelled to homeschool Oscar while the district looked for a classroom that could meet his unique needs. Day after day, I tried to educate an ADHD four-year-old. Day after day, I'd fall into bed, feeling as if I had failed.

After eight exhausting months of homeschooling, our public school district still hadn't secured him a spot or offered so much as a single appropriate compensatory service, and so Arran and I felt we had no choice but to enroll him at a private Waldorf school for children with sensory differences and learning challenges. Thus began a long and costly process of suing our local public school district for tuition reimbursement. We could barely afford it, but I finally felt like I was advocating for my child.

Some weeks after we enrolled Oscar at his new school, I had dinner with some friends. Their kids were at the public preschool our son had been kicked out of. I sat in silence while they complained about the Twix Rice Krispie Treats the teachers handed out as a snack, speculating that the company providing the food was the same one that serviced prisons.

"I suppose your son eats quinoa for a snack," Natalie said, and laughed nervously.

I smiled, just as awkwardly, because he did, actually. Every Tuesday. On the other days of the week, the school serves millet, porridge, freshly baked bread, and homemade soup. After snack time,

Oscar feeds the chickens. At a Waldorf school, academics are delayed until age seven, special needs or not. He and his classmates spend most of their day climbing trees and making art.

If she could afford it, Natalie tells me, she'd have chosen a Waldorf school for her son, who also has sensory needs.

Mele would thrive at a school like Oscar's, I thought. But he could function in a typical one. Behavior charts motivate him, whereas these same interventions make my son anxious, which, in turn, triggers him to fight or run.

In this moment, I felt misunderstood. I felt ashamed—of my son, of our choices. I felt defensive. I felt angry. Most people, I realized, do not understand our plight. Natalie had no idea how I felt in this moment, how I often feel: like a pariah. The physical, emotional, and mental—not to mention financial—stress of raising a child with a disability, why, I think, *they have no idea.* The anger returns. I remind myself I have no idea what she is going through either. In these moments when it is tempting to harden to my own pain, I remind myself that we have no idea what another person has been through. Even when we do, we don't.

The most important part of friendship, I think, is forgiveness. A willingness to witness one another's journey is the cornerstone of shame-resilient friendships. It means recognizing your humanity, regardless of what's on the outside. You don't need to be perfect, but you must be willing to be vulnerable, do the work, and remain emotionally honest. Emotional intelligence means learning to pay attention to your triggers and being sensitive to other people's triggers as well. As *Platonic* author Marisa G. Franco put it, "We don't heal shame by hiding it."

The first step, always, is bringing uncomfortable truths to light.

I am working to forgive others, just as I practice forgiving myself. I am learning to love and appreciate people for who they are and what they can offer, however imperfectly. Offer what you can—and when you can't, that's okay. It has to be.

We Are the Threat—But We Are Also the Cure

Even before the COVID-19 pandemic cut off so many of us from friends, loved ones, and support systems, the US Surgeon General reported that as many as one in two adults in America reported experiencing loneliness. It's more than just a terrible feeling, the 2023 report made clear. A lack of intimacy and connection leads to pain, injury and loss, grief, fear, fatigue, and exhaustion. The mortality impact of being socially disconnected is similar to that caused by smoking fifteen cigarettes a day.

What's worse, we feel ashamed of our loneliness.

"It's ironic," blogger Stephan Joppich writes. "Having researched, explored, and experienced loneliness for years, I should know there's nothing to be ashamed of. I should know that, in many countries, more than half of the population feels lonely regularly. I should know that loneliness is an inherently human emotion.

"And yet," he goes on, "the stigma of loneliness seems to be tattooed on my synapses. During the loneliest periods of my life, the L-word felt smeared on my forehead like a bold, flashy warning sign. I was constantly terrified of people finding out about my isolation, of being called a lonely loser."

I know how this feels. I wouldn't wish this pain on my worst enemy.

These days, I don't have very many "enemies"—that is, I like to believe I don't harbor ill feelings toward anyone. During the course of reporting this book, however, I discovered a pain point.

A year after I was dubbed "the hooker teacher," and I'd established myself as a writing instructor and was teaching writing to adults, a reporter from the *New York Post* signed up as a student in my memoir-writing workshop so that she could write a "news article" on what I was up to: "Fmr. Prostitute and Stripper Is Back in the Classroom as Writing Instructor."

"She's a working girl once again!" the hit piece began.

That reporter, Tara Palmeri, went on some years later to become the White House correspondent for ABC News and an investigative journalist with a focus on covering stories related to sexual assault and abuse. For a long time, I hate-followed her career. Even though I knew better. Even though it didn't feel good. Even though I knew that hating her meant there was a corner of myself I still wasn't happy with.

I didn't want to feel that way anymore, not toward anyone. And so in the midst of my researching this book, I direct messaged her on Instagram. I reminded her who I was and asked if we could talk.

To her credit, she said yes.

For the most part, she did a good job of owning her part. In the beginning, it felt a bit like she was fawning ("You know, I actually found your class to be really useful. And I thought you were really great. And I don't quote you at all in this . . . I wasn't surreptitiously recording.") And there was a little "all's well that ends well" in reference to this book (as if the opportunity had been handed to me thanks to the *New York Post*).

I accepted her apology, but didn't really feel as if anything was going to be repaired. Then Tara started telling me her story. "This isn't to make excuses," she began, "but like, you know, my first job"—an internship, she explained—"I was making like, $15 an hour. I couldn't afford an apartment. Before that, I actually worked in a nightclub, not sex work, but . . . it was not great." From there, Tara talked about how she was a first-generation American and the first person in her family to go to college, and how she ended up working for the *New York Post*. "It was my first *real* job," Tara said. She described what an opportunity that was—but also how shitty it felt to work there, particularly as a woman.

They had just moved her from Page Six to the news desk. "The news desk, they really didn't want me. In fact, I [later] heard they were like planning to fire me at that point. I had no idea then. But they were hazing me so bad. And I was just so miserable. I had an ulcer, I was so miserable. And then they had this assignment for me to go listen and follow you and your new job of teaching adults.

"I hated having to do it, but I did it," she said.

"Working in a tabloid where you do things because you're told to do them. And you do what you're told, because that's how you live. That's how you make money. That's how you survive."

Tara reminds me she was just twenty-five years old then, and that she didn't have very much self-confidence.

"Not to make excuses," she says again. "Just to explain where I was when I wrote that story. And I understand that it hurt you. I've thought about it before, actually, before you even reached out to me, because I saw you had written online about it." Before reading those heartfelt personal essays, she says, "I didn't realize that [my actions] had that kind of impact on you."

As Tara talked, I softened. I could empathize. Of course I could! Who couldn't? What woman doesn't know what it's like to work for mostly men, and to endure abuse? We've all felt the queasy shame that comes from compromising our morals and falling short of our ideals. When Tara says she did it because she felt she had to, I get it.

Since then, Tara says, there've been times she's said no.

Tara tells me about working for women and feeling taken care of. One mentor in particular—"She looked after me, and my career thrived.

"Every time in my life when I feel like there's a woman looking out for me, I've done so much better. And all the times in my life when I've had men managing me? I haven't thrived. We are animals that are fearful. We worry about resources, we worry about protecting ourselves. I mean, I've had women that have sabotaged me, too. And I look at them. And I kind of feel bad for them. They were coming at it from a place of fear and insecurity. . . . I don't hold grudges."

Neither do I.

Yes, I have been hurt. And I can—make that will—be hurt again. Shame is inevitable, especially so long as I allow myself to be vulnerable. Yes, people are the threat. But they are also the cure. Conversations like the one I had with Tara, and everyone I talked to for the purpose of writing this book, are my medicine. If I could teach my children only one lesson, it is this: no one, no matter how strong they are, can go it alone.

I see myself so much in my daughter. Her desire to be beautiful. Her obsession, already, with being *good*. When it comes to our appearance, we internalized society's definition of beautiful well before we had any idea of who we actually were—and now, for some of us, our lives are halfway over. But it's not too late. We can do the work. And we must. It is time to look beyond what we've been taught to focus on at the exclusion of all else.

Ultimately, to reconnect with the world, and ourselves, we must connect with other women—even when it's hard. We must learn to love by loving.

No matter what, I teach my daughter: tell the truth.

It will save your life.

For Further Reading

Sara Ahmed. *The Promise of Happiness*. Durham, NC: Duke University Press, 2010.

Katherine Angel. *Daddy Issues: Love and Hate in the Time of Patriarchy*. London: Peninsula Press, 2019.

Lisa Feldman Barrett. *How Emotions Are Made: The Secret Life of the Brain*. New York: Houghton Mifflin Harcourt, 2017.

Tara Brach. *Radical Acceptance: Embracing Your Life with the Heart of a Buddha*. New York: Bantam, 2004.

Kim Brooks. *Small Animals: Parenthood in the Age of Fear*. New York: Flatiron Books, 2018.

Brené Brown. *Daring Greatly: How the Courage to Be Vulnerable Transforms the Way We Live, Love, Parent, and Lead*. New York: Avery, 2015.

Brené Brown. *The Gifts of Imperfection: Let Go of Who You Think You're Supposed to Be and Embrace Who You Are*. Center City, MO: Hazelden, 2010.

Brené Brown. *Women & Shame: Reaching Out, Speaking Truths and Building Connection*. Austin, TX: 3C Press, 2004.

Tarana Burke and Brené Brown, eds. *You Are Your Best Thing: Vulnerability, Shame Resilience, and the Black Experience*. New York: Random House, 2021.

Tarana Burke. *Unbound: My Story of Liberation and the Birth of the Me Too Movement*. New York: Flatiron Books, 2021.

Pema Chödrön. *When Things Fall Apart: Heart Advice for Difficult Times* (Anniversary Edition). Boulder, CO: Shambhala, 2016.

Melissa Febos. *Girlhood*. New York: Bloomsbury, 2022.

Angela Garbes. *Essential Labor: Mothering as Social Change*. New York: Harper Wave, 2022.

Arline T. Geronimus. *Weathering: The Extraordinary Stress of Ordinary Life in an Unjust Society*. New York: Little, Brown Spark, 2023.

Anna Goldfarb. *Modern Friendship: How to Nurture Our Most Valued Connections*. Louisville, CO: Sounds True, 2024.

Shira Hassan. *Saving Our Own Lives: A Liberatory Practice of Harm Reduction*. Chicago: Haymarket Books, 2022.

Judith L. Herman. *Trauma and Recovery: The Aftermath of Violence—from Domestic Abuse to Political Terror*. New York: Basic Books, 1997.

Marjorie Ingall and Susan McCarthy. *Sorry, Sorry, Sorry: The Case for Good Apologies*. New York: Gallery Books, 2023.

Erin Khar. *Strung Out: One Last Hit and Other Lies That Nearly Killed Me*. New York: Park Row, 2020.

Peter Lovenheim. *In the Neighborhood: The Search for Community on an American Street, One Sleepover at a Time*. New York: TarcherPerigee, 2011.

Gabor Maté. *When the Body Says No: The Cost of Hidden Stress*. Toronto, ON: Vintage Canada, 2004.

Amanda Montei. *Touched Out: Motherhood, Misogyny, Consent, and Control.* Boston: Beacon Press, 2023.

Cathy O'Neil. *The Shame Machine: Who Profits in the New Age of Humiliation.* New York: Crown, 2022.

Sara Petersen. *Momfluenced: Inside the Maddening, Picture-Perfect World of Mommy Influencer Culture.* Boston: Beacon Press, 2023.

Eve Rodsky. *Fair Play: A Game-Changing Solution for When You Have Too Much to Do (and More Life to Live).* New York: G. P. Putnam's Sons, 2019.

Dave Runyon. *The Art of Neighboring: Building Genuine Relationships Right Outside Your Door.* Grand Rapids, MI: Baker Books, 2012.

Sonya Renee Taylor. *The Body Is Not an Apology: The Power of Radical Self-Love.* Oakland, CA: Berrett–Koehler Publishers, Inc., 2018.

Bessel van der Kolk. *The Body Keeps the Score: Brain, Mind, and Body in the Healing of Trauma.* New York: Penguin Books, 2014.

Acknowledgments

Thank you to my agent, Laura Mazer, for insisting I was more than *that* story. Michelle Howry, and the whole team at Putnam: I am so grateful to you for recognizing this project's potential and helping to usher it into the world. To everyone I interviewed, thank you for entrusting me with your stories. We all owe this book to the professionals who help raise my children: Jeanette Rodriguez, Chela Crane, and everyone else at the Otto Specht School—especially Oscar's one-on-ones: Tristen, Alan, Amanda, Ariel, and Mandel—as well as Alan Berger, Elisa Cordero, and all the folks at Peace Through Play. Thanks to my besties, Christa Lynch and Reema Zhar. Thanks to Mariah and Rose, for letting me sleep in a van in your driveway. Thank you to Threefold Café, Harvest Moon, and Leigh and Mathew at Hungry Hollow Co-op, you kept me company and kept me fed. Shout-out to Peekskill Coffee House, Kurzhal Coffee, and all the other coffee shops that didn't kick me out, all the way back to Joe Coffee on Thirteenth Street. I am especially grateful to the writers who've supported me throughout this project: Erin Khar, Debbie Weingarten, Lauren DePino, Natalka Burian, Simone Gorrindo, Elisabeth Fairfield Stokes, Karie Fugett, and all the other "sulky bitches," as well as my accountability club, Anna Goldfarb and Cece

Xie. Other writers and industry professionals who've lit the way include Jami Attenberg, Kim Brooks, Lily Burana, Jancee Dunn, Melissa Febos, Isaac Fitzgerald, Nick Flynn, Ashley C. Ford, Roxane Gay, Emily Gould, Gemma Hartley, Pete Hausler, Stephanie Land, Kiese Laymon, Betsy Lerner, Janet Mock, Abigail Pesta, Elissa Schappell, Ted Scheinman, Mandy Stadtmiller, Saba Sulaiman Meredith Talusan Hanson, Jia Tolentino, and Rebecca Traister. Very special thank you to Alex Steele, Dana Miller, and Kelly Caldwell at Gotham Writers Workshop, and Aaron Zimmerman at NY Writers Coalition. I love you, Karen Ladson. Thank you, Brie. Thank you, Gloria Allred. I am grateful to my instructors at The New School and Antioch College, especially my adviser, Cheryl Keen. Thank you to the Authors League Fund, PEN America, and the Haven Foundation for your financial support. NYC 12 Step and Dharma Punx: You saved my life. Arran, Oscar, and Molly: You give it meaning. Last but not least, let this book, and the fact that it finally (finally!) made it into the world, be a message for my students to believe in your story, and never give up.

Index